Fanny Barry

Soap-Bubble Stories

For Children

Fanny Barry

Soap-Bubble Stories
For Children

ISBN/EAN: 9783337004859

Printed in Europe, USA, Canada, Australia, Japan

Cover: Foto ©Thomas Meinert / pixelio.de

More available books at **www.hansebooks.com**

Soap = Bubble Stories.

FOR CHILDREN.

BY

FANNY BARRY,

AUTHOR OF "THE FOX FAMILY," "THE OBSTINATE ELM LEAF," "THE BEARS OF WUNDERMERK," ETC.

New York:

JAMES POTT & CO., 14 & 16, ASTOR PLACE.

1892.

To

VERA, ELSIE,

OSKAR, OLGA, ERIK,

NEVA, JESSIE,

LEO, DOROTHY, CLAUDE,

AND

HERBERT.

IT was twilight, and the children, tired of playing, gathered round the fire.

Outside, the snow fell softly, softly ; and the bare trees shook their branches in the keen air. The pleasant glow of the blazing logs lighted up the circle of happy faces, and peopled the distant corners with elfin shadows.

All the afternoon the children, pipe in hand, with soap suds before them, had been blowing airy bubbles that caught the gleams of a hundred flying rainbows—but now in the fading daylight, the pipes were put aside, and they threw themselves down on the fur rug, and looked with thoughtful eyes into the caverns of the fire.

"What can we do now?" they cried, "Won't *you* make us some bubbles?"

And someone sitting in the shadow, who had watched and admired their handiwork : whipped up some white froth in a fairy basin, and taking a pipe, she blew them some bubbles.

Not so beautiful as the children's own, with their pure reflections of the light and sunshine—but the best she could fashion with the materials she had at hand ; for the only soap she could find was Imagination, and her pipe was a humble black pen.

Contents.

x.

The Troll in the Church Fountain.

CHAPTER I.

IT was a village of fountains. They poured from the sides of houses, bubbled up at street corners, sprang from stone troughs by the roadside, and one even gushed from the very walls of the old Church itself, and fell with a monotonous tinkle into a carved stone basin beneath.

The old Church stood on a high plateau overlooking the lake. It jutted out so far, on its great rock, that it seemed to overhang the precipice; and as the neighbours walked upon the terrace on Sundays, and enjoyed the shade of the row of plane trees, they could look down over the low walls of the Churchyard almost into the chimneys of the wooden houses clustering below.

There were wide stone seats on the terrace, grey and worn by the weather, and by the generations of children who had played round them; and here the mothers and grandmothers, with their distaffs in their hands, loved to collect on summer evenings.

Often Terli had seen them from his home by the mountain

A

torrent, for he was so high up, he looked down upon the whole village; and he had often longed to join them and hear what they were saying; but as he was nothing but a River-Troll, he was not able to venture within sight or sound of the water of the holy Church Fountain.

Anywhere else he was free to roam; teazing the children, worrying the women as they washed their clothes at the open stone basins, even putting his lean fingers into the fountain spout to stop the water, while the people remained staring open-mouthed, or ran off to fetch a neighbour to find out what was the matter.

This was all very pleasant to Terli, and at night he would hurry back to his relations in their cave under the stones of the torrent, and enjoy a good laugh at the day's adventures.

There was only one thing that worried him. Several of the cleverest old women of the village, who had on several occasions seen Terli dancing about the country, agreed to hang a little pot of the Church water in the doors of their houses; and once or twice the Troll, on attempting to enter in order to teaze the inhabitants, had suddenly caught sight of the water, and rushed away with a scream of rage and disappointment.

"Never River-Troll can stand the sight of the Church Fountain!" said the old women, and rubbed their hands gleefully.

In the early summer there was to be a great wedding at

the old Church, the Bridegroom the son of a rich farmer, the Bride one of the young girls of the village; and Terli, who had known them both from childhood, determined that for once in his life he would enter the unknown region of the Church Terrace.

"Elena has often annoyed me in the past," laughed Terli, "so it is only fair I should try and annoy her in the future"—and he sat down cross-legged at the bottom of a water trough to arrange his plans quietly in seclusion.

An old horse came by, dragging a creaking waggon, and the driver stopped to allow the animal to drink.

The Troll raised himself leisurely, and as the horse put in his head, Terli seized it in both hands, and hung on so firmly that it was impossible for the poor creature to get away.

"Let go!" said the horse, angrily—for he understood the Troll language. "Let me go! What are you doing?"

"I shan't let you go till you make me a promise. You get the Wood-Troll to cork up the Church Fountain at daybreak on Friday morning, and I'll let you drink as much as you like now, and go without hindrance afterwards."

"I shan't promise," said the horse, crossly. "I don't see why I should."

"Well, I shall hang on till you *do*," said the Troll with a disagreeable laugh; and he gripped the old horse more tightly than ever.

"Oh, leave off! I'm being suffocated. I'll promise anything," cried the horse.

"'LET GO!' SAID THE HORSE, ANGRILY, 'LET ME GO! WHAT ARE YOU DOING?'"

Terli withdrew his hands immediately, sinking down to the bottom of the trough with a chuckle that made the water bubble furiously; and the old horse, without waiting to drink, trotted off with an activity that surprised his master.

"Remember your promise!" called the Troll, putting his head suddenly over the edge of the trough, and pointing a thin finger. "On Friday at daybreak the Church Fountain stopped, or you don't drink comfortably for a twelve-month!"

CHAPTER II.

Early on Friday morning the bridal procession started gaily, and all the village folks were so occupied they never noticed that the Church Fountain had ceased to bubble.

The bells rang out ; while the Troll, hidden in the branches of a tree close to the entrance door, glanced first at the procession and then at a wedge of wood sticking out of the stone mouth of the Fountain, and he laughed elfishly.

" Ha, ha ! The old horse has kept his promise. This *is* seeing the world," he whispered triumphantly.

The marriage ceremony was soon over, and as the newly-wedded pair stepped out upon the terrace again, Terli drew from his pocket a little jar of water, and *splash!* fell some drops from it right in the eyes of the Bride and Bridegroom.

" It is beginning to rain ! I saw the clouds gathering ! Run, run, for the nearest shelter!" cried everyone confusedly, and off dashed the crowd, panting and breathless.

Now it was an unfortunate thing, that after the wedding everything in the new household seemed to go wrong.

" The young people have had their heads turned," whispered the old women, and the poor Bride looked pale and disconsolate.

" It is a wretched house to have married into," she said to her mother. " Nothing but these poor boards for furniture, no good fields or garden—all so dull and disagreeable ;

and then my husband—he seems always discontented. I think I was happier at home;" and she tapped her foot impatiently.

Her mother argued and remonstrated, and at last began to weep bitterly.

"You must be bewitched, Elena, to complain like this! You have everything a reasonable girl can wish for."

"Everything? Why I have *nothing!*" cried Elena angrily, and ran from the room; leaving Terli, who was hiding in a water-bucket, to stamp his feet with delight.

"Ha! ha! it is going on excellently," he shouted in his little cracked voice. "Once let them have the water from the Trolls' well in their eyes, they'll never be contented again!" and he upset the bucket in which he was standing over the feet of the Bride's mother, who had to run home hastily to change her wet shoes.

"This is the work of the River-Trolls, I believe," she said to herself, as she held up her soaked skirts carefully. "I'll find out all about it on St. John's Eve, if I can't do so before"—and she nodded angrily towards the mountain torrent.

Days passed, and the sad temper of the newly-married couple did not improve.

They scarcely attempted to speak to each other, and groaned so much over the hardships of their life, that all their friends became tired of trying to comfort them.

"They're bewitched," said the Bride's mother, "bewitched,

and nothing else. But wait till St. John's Eve, and you'll
see I shall cure them."

She spoke mysteriously, but as she was a sensible woman
everyone believed her.

On St. John's Eve—as I daresay you know—all animals
have the power of talking together like human beings, and
punctually as the clock struck twelve the Bride's mother put
on her thick shoes, and taking the stable lantern from its
nail, she went off to the stable, refusing to allow either her
husband or son to accompany her.

As she entered the door of the outhouse, she heard the
oxen already whispering to each other, and the old horse,
with his head over the division, addressing friendly remarks
to a family of goats close by.

" Do you know anything of Terli or the Wood-Trolls ? "
enquired the old woman, looking at the oxen severely.

" No, no, no ! " and they shook their heads slowly.

The Bride's mother then repeated her question to the goat
family, who denied any knowledge of the Trolls with a series
of terrified bleats.

" There is only *you*, then," said the Bride's mother to the
old horse. " You have served us faithfully, and we have
been kind masters to you. Tell me : do you know anything
of Terli or the Wood-Trolls ? "

" I do," said the old horse with dignity. " I can tell you
more than anyone else dreams of;" and he stepped from
his stall with an air of the greatest importance.

The old woman sat down upon an upturned stable-bucket, and prepared to listen.

"Just before the wedding," commenced the horse, "I was passing through the village with old master, when we stopped to drink. No sooner had I got my nose into the Fountain than, *heuw!* Terli had hold of me, and not an inch would he loosen his grip till I promised to let him see the wedding by getting the Wood-Trolls to stop up the Church Fountain. What was I to do? I was forced to agree, and from that promise comes all the misery of the Bride and Bridegroom."

The old horse then went on to explain what Terli had done on the wedding day, while the Bride's mother jumped up from the water-bucket with a cry of delight.

"All will be well now. You have done us the greatest possible service, and shall live in leisure for the rest of your life," she said; and ran out of the stables towards the house, before the astonished animals could recover themselves.

"I've found it all out," she cried to her husband. "Now all we have to do is to catch Terli."

"Not so easy, wife," said the Bride's father, but the old woman smiled in a mysterious manner.

"Leave it to me, husband, *I* shall manage it. Our children will be happy again to-morrow, you will see."

CHAPTER III.

The next day at sunrise, the Bride's mother crept off secretly to the Church Fountain and brought back a large pailful of the water. This she emptied into a wash-tub, and covered with some green pine branches, and on the top of all she placed a wooden bowl half filled with butter-milk.

"Terli likes it so much—he will do anything for butter-milk," she said to herself, as she propped open the kitchen door, and went off with a light heart to see her daughter.

She carried with her a jug of the Church water, and when she arrived at the farm house, she gave it to her daughter and son-in-law, and begged them to bathe their eyes with it immediately.

With much grumbling they obeyed her; but what a change occurred directly they had done so!

The day, which had seemed cloudy and threatening rain, now appeared bright and hopeful. The Bride ran over her new house with exclamations of delight at all the comfortable arrangements, and the Bridegroom declared he was a lucky man to have married a good wife, and have a farm that anyone might reasonably be proud of!

"How could we ever have troubled over anything?" said the young Bride, "I can't understand it! We are young, and we are happy."

The old woman smiled wisely. "It was only the Troll's

well-water, " she said, and went home as fast as her feet
would carry her.

As she neared her own door, she heard sounds of splashing

"TAKE ME OUT! TAKE ME OUT! IT GIVES ME THE TOOTH-ACHE!"

and screaming in a shrill piping voice ; and on entering, saw
Terli struggling violently in the tub of Church water, the
little bowl of buttermilk lying spilt upon the floor.

" Take me out ! Take me out! It gives me the tooth-ache !"
wailed the Troll, but the Bride's mother was a wise woman,
and determined that now she had caught their tormentor she
would keep him safely.

" I've got the toothache in every joint!" shouted Terli.
" Let me out, and I'll *never* tease you any more."

" It serves you very well right," said the old woman, and
she poured the contents of the tub—including Terli—into a
large bucket, and carried it off in triumph to the Church
Fountain.

Here she emptied the bucket into the carved stone basin,
and left Terli kicking and screaming, while she went home
to the farmhouse to breakfast.

" That's a good morning's work, wife ; if you never do
another :" said the Bride's father, who had come into the
kitchen just as Terli upset the bowl of butter-milk, and fell
through the pine branches headlong into the tub beneath.
" We shall live in peace and quietness now, for Terli was
the most mischievous of the whole of the Troll-folk."

The words of the Bride's father proved to be quite true,
for after the capture of the Water-Troll the village enjoyed
many years of quietness and contentment.

As to Terli, he lived in great unhappiness in the Church
Fountain; enduring a terrible series of tooth-aches, but
unable to escape from the magic power of the water.

At the end of that time, however, a falling tree split the
sides of the carved stone basin into fragments, and the

Troll, escaping with the water which flowed out, darted from the Churchyard and safely reached his old home in the bed of the mountain torrent.

" The Church Fountain is broken, and Terli has escaped," said the good folks the next morning—and the old people shook their heads gravely, in alarm—but I suppose Terli had had a good lesson, for he never troubled the village any more.

The Imp in the Chintz Curtain.

E was a wicked-looking Imp, and he lived in a bed curtain.

No one knew he was in the house, not even the master and mistress. The little girl who slept in the chintz-curtained bed was the only person who knew of his existence, and she never mentioned him, even to her old nurse.

She had made his acquaintance one Christmas Eve, as she lay awake, trying to keep her tired eyes open long enough to see Santa Klaus come down the chimney. The Imp sprang into view with a *cr-r-r-ick, cr-r-r-ack* of falling wood in the great fireplace, and there he stood bowing to Marianne from the left-hand corner of the chintz curtain.

A green leaf formed his hat, some straggling branches his feet; his thin body was a single rose-stem, and his red face a crumpled rose-bud.

A flaw in the printing of the chintz curtain had given him life—a life distinct from that of the other rose leaves.

" You're lying awake very late to-night—what's that for ? " he enquired, shaking the leaf he wore upon his head, and looking at Marianne searchingly.

"Why, don't you see I'm waiting for Santa Klaus?" replied Marianne. "I've always missed him before, but this time *nothing* shall make me go to sleep!" She sat up in bed and opened her eyes as widely as possible.

"He has generally been here before this," said the Imp. "I can remember your great-aunt sleeping in this very bed and being in just the same fuss. I got down and danced about all night, and she thought I was earwigs."

"*I* should never think you were an earwig—you're too pink and green—but don't talk, I can hear something buzzing."

"Santa Klaus doesn't buzz," said the Chintz Imp. "He comes down *flop!* Once in your aunt's time, I knew him nearly stick in the chimney. He had too many things in his sack. You should have heard how he struggled, it was like thunder! Everyone said how high the wind was."

"I hope he won't do it to-night," said Marianne, "I could never pull him down by myself!"

As she spoke the room seemed to be violently shaken, and there was a sound of falling plaster, followed by some loud kicks.

"Whew—w!" cried the Chintz Imp, "he's done it again!"

Marianne started up in great excitement. She sprang from her bed, and ran towards the old-fashioned fireplace.

Nothing was at first to be seen; but as the fire had died down to a few hot embers, Marianne could, by craning her head forwards, look right up into the misty darkness of the great chimney.

There, to her astonishment, she saw a pair of large brown-covered feet hanging down helplessly; while a deep voice from above cried—

"Get me out of this, or I shall break down the chimney!"

"Oh, what *am* I to do?" exclaimed Marianne anxiously, "I'm not tall enough to reach you! Shall I fetch my Aunt Olga, or would you prefer my old nurse?"

"Certainly not," said the voice, with decision. "I have never been seen by a grown-up person, and I don't intend to begin now. Either you must get me down by yourself, or I shall manage to work out at the top again—and then I'm sorry to say you'll have to go without your presents."

Marianne sat down on the hearthrug in a state of anxious consideration. There waved the great brown feet, and two or three steps would land them safely on the hearthrug, but how could it possibly be managed?

The Chintz Imp curled up his green legs and sat down beside her, his bright red eyes blinking thoughtfully.

"We must hang on to him," he said at last; "or what do you say to my trying to collect a dozen or so children, to pull?"

"Why they'd all be in bed hours ago," said Marianne. "Besides, their parents would never let them come, and Uncle Max would want to know whatever we were doing."

"Yes. I see *that* idea is no good. Have you such a thing as a pocket-knife?" enquired the Chintz Imp.

"A beauty," said Marianne; "four blades, a button-hook, and a corkscrew."

"Ah, the corkscrew might be of some use if we could draw him out with it; but he might object. However, I'll try what I can do with the knife."

"You won't cut him! You'll have to be very careful!"

"Of course," said the Chintz Imp. "Do you think I am as old as your great-aunt, without knowing much more than *you* do! Bring me the knife. I'm going to swarm up the chimney and scratch away the mortar. Leave it entirely to me, and Santa Klaus will be down here in an hour or two!"

Marianne ran off to her little play box, and returned with the knife. It was almost as large as the Chintz Imp, but he possessed so much wiry strength in his thin arms and backbone that he was able to clamber up the chimney without difficulty.

"Are you all right?" cried Marianne, standing with her bare feet on the edge of the stone fender, and holding up the night-light as high as she could without singeing Santa Klaus.

"Getting up," replied the Chintz Imp, "but he's in very tight!"

"Is it his sack that's stuck?" enquired Marianne, anxiously.

"Yes, yes! It's only my sack!" cried the deep voice;

"you get that loose, and I shall drop into the room like a fairy."

Marianne strained her eyes up the chimney, but could see nothing.

"Take care! Here's a lot of plaster falling!"

The warning was just in time, for, as Marianne's head disappeared, a handful of cement fell rattling into the fireplace, just escaping her bare feet as she jumped on to the hearthrug.

"The knife does beautifully," cried the voice of the Chintz Imp. "I think when I've loosened this paint box, he'll fall down immediately."

"Oh, do be careful!" said Marianne. "A paint box is what I've been longing for! Don't chip it if you can possibly help it!"

"Of course I shan't," replied the Chintz Imp. "If he wouldn't kick so much, I should get him out in half the time."

"I'm not kicking," cried Santa Klaus's voice indignantly. "I've been as still as a rock, even with that horrid penknife close to my ear the whole time."

"Have a little patience," said the Chintz Imp soothingly. "I promise not to hurt you."

Marianne began to feel very cold. The excitement, so far, had buoyed her up; but now the monotonous *chip, chipping* of the Chintz Imp continued so long that she jumped into her chintz-curtained bed, determined to stay there until something new and interesting called her up again.

B

"I can't do any good, so I may as well be comfortable," she thought, and pulled the eider-down quilt up to her chin luxuriously.

"I *hope* he'll get out! It *would* be a disappointment to have that paint-box taken away again. Perhaps it would be given to someone who wouldn't care for it. I wonder if it's tin, with moist colours? I must ask Uncle Max to have that chimney made wider——" At this point Marianne's eyes closed and she fell asleep.

She was awakened by a loud *thump!* that seemed to shake the very bed in which she was lying; and as she sprang up in a state of great excitement, she saw Santa Klaus picking himself up from the hearthrug on which he had apparently fallen with great violence.

"Oh dear!" cried Marianne, "I hope you are not hurt? How careless of the Chintz Imp to throw you down like that!"

"It was no one's fault but my own," said Santa Klaus as he dusted the remains of soot and plaster off his brown cloak. "I should have remembered my experience with your great-aunt, but I knew how much you wanted that paint-box," and he slipped into Marianne's stocking a japanned box with a whole sheaf of paint brushes.

"Oh, thank you, Santa Klaus! You can't think how I've wished for it; my own is such a horrid little thing. And those beautiful pictures for my scrap-book, and the things for the doll's house—and I *really* believe that's the book of fairy tales I've been longing for for months!"

Marianne's face shone with delighted expectation as she opened the top of her stocking and peeped in.

"Not till the morning," cried Santa Klaus; "you know my rule," and patting Marianne on the head, he disappeared, with his sack much lightened, up the chimney.

"Oh, do come here!" cried Marianne to the Chintz Imp. "I must talk to somebody."

"I think you certainly *ought* to talk to me," said the Chintz Imp, coming carefully down the brickwork, hand over hand, and laying the knife down in the fender. "Without me you wouldn't have had a single present."

"Of course, I'm very grateful," said Marianne. "I wish he had brought you something, though I'm sure I don't know what would be useful to you."

"Well, I should like a good many things," replied the Chintz Imp, perching himself on a brass knob at the end of the bedstead, "and one or two I think you can get me easily. I'm tired of this room and the little society I see, and I long for the great world. Can't you get me put on a settee in the Servants' Hall, or somewhere lively?"

"I'll ask Aunt Olga," said Marianne. "She promised me a Christmas present, and I was to choose. Suppose I choose new bed curtains?"

"Certainly," said the Chintz Imp, "but be sure you bargain to hang me in some cheerful place. Sixty years in one room is too much of a good thing—I want a change!" and he stretched himself wearily.

" I really will do my best for you," said Marianne. " I'm
afraid you're too faded for the drawing-room, but I won't
have new curtains until I can see you put somewhere nice.
I suppose you wouldn't like the passages ? "

" Decidedly not," replied the Chintz Imp. " Dull places.
No fun, and nothing going on. The Servants' Hall, or stay
where I am!" He folded his green arms with determination.

"I'm sure I can manage it," said Marianne, and fell asleep
again while she was arranging the words in which she should
make the suggestion to Aunt Olga.

The next day Marianne awoke betimes, and immediately
inspected the contents of her stocking.

There, stuffed clumsily inside it, was everything she had
been wishing for during the year, and more too !

" Do come and look at my things ! " cried Marianne to the
Chintz Imp, but he remained rigidly against his shiny
spotted background and refused to move, though Marianne
thought she saw a twinkle in his eye, which showed he was
not quite so impassive as he appeared to be.

" I'll try and get him put into the Servants' Hall as soon
as possible," she thought. " It makes me quite nervous to
think he may pounce upon me any minute. Besides, one
must keep one's promises ! How extraordinary it is he can
make himself so perfectly flat."

As soon as she was dressed she ran down to the dining
room.

" Dear Aunt Olga, I've got such quantities of things to

show you!" she cried, "and as you said I might choose, may I please have new chintz to my bed, and no pattern on it, so that it can't come out and be Imps—I mean, have funny shapes on it. And may my old curtains be put in the Servants' Hall? He says it will be more cheerful for him, and though, of course, he's been very kind to me, I think I would rather he went somewhere else. Besides, it *is* dull for him up there, all by himself—I mean, it would be dull for *any* kind of chintz."

"I do think Santa Klaus has got into your head, Marianne!" said Aunt Olga, laughing; but she promised to buy the new curtains.

In course of time they arrived—the palest blue, with little harmless frillings to them; and the old chintz was carried off to the Servants' Hall to make a box cover.

There it still hangs, and if you stoop down and examine it closely, you will see the Chintz Imp looking more lively than ever, with his green hat on one side, and a twinkling red eye on the watch for any sort of amusement.

Marianne often goes to see him, but, rather to her disappointment, he looks the other way, and appears not to recognize her.

"Perhaps it's just as well," she says to herself, "for he seems very happy, and if the servants knew he was here I believe they would turn him out immediately."

Heartsease.

THE three-cornered scrap of garden by the elm tree, with a border of stones, and a neat trodden path down the middle, belonged to little Bethea.

It grew things in a most wonderful way. Stocks and marigolds, primroses and lupines, Canterbury bells and lavender: all came out at their different seasons, and all flourished—for Bethea watered and tended them so faithfully that they loved her.

On a soft spring day Bethea stood by her garden with scissors and basket, snipping away at the brightest and best of her children; carefully, so that she might not hurt them, and with judgment, so that they might bloom again when they wished to.

"Do you know where you're going?" she said—"To the Hospital. Grandmamma's going to take me, and you're being gathered to cheer up the sick people there—aren't you pleased?" And the flowers nodded.

"I don't suppose I shall be picked. I don't think I'm good enough!" whispered a very small purple pansy, who had only recently been planted, to a beetle who happened to be

"BETHEA WATERED AND TENDED THEM SO FAITHFULLY THAT THEY LOVED HER."

crawling by. " I should like to go with the others, though I don't suppose it would cheer anyone to see me, I'm not light enough ! "

" Don't be too sure," said the beetle solidly. " You've a nice velvety softness about you, and then you have the best name of them all. What sick person wouldn't like to have Heartsease ? "

" I think I've got enough now," said Bethea, as she laid the last primula in her basket.

"Oh, do take me !" cried the pansy, touching her little brown shoe with one of its leaves to attract her attention, " I do want to help !" and Bethea stooped down, she scarcely knew why, gathered it, and put it with the rest of her flowers.

The drive to the Hospital was along a dusty country road, and the flowers under their paper covering, gasped for breath.

As soon as they arrived, Bethea, following her grand-mother, carried them up to the room where children were lying in the little white beds, and gave them to the woman who was in charge of it.

" Please would you mind putting them in water for the children," she said in her soft voice, and the woman smiled and nodded.

Bethea took a few of the flowers out, and went round to the different beds offering one or two, shyly, until she came to a thin pale boy—a new patient, whom she had never seen before.

"He's only been here a fortnight," said the woman in a whisper, "and we can't get him to take any interest in anything—I don't know what we're going to do with him!"

"Is he very ill?" asked Bethea, wistfully.

"No, not so bad as some. A crooked leg, that will get well in time if only we can wake him up a little."

"I'm so sorry I have nothing but this flower left," said Bethea, as she stooped over the boy's curly head, and gave him the small purple pansy.

"Oh, I wish I was more beautiful!" sighed the little dark flower. "*Now* would be an opportunity to do some good in the world!"

The boy turned wearily, but his face lighted up as he saw the pansy. His eyes brightened and he seized it eagerly.

"Heartsease! Oh, it's like home. We've lots of that growing in our garden. I always had some on Sundays!" he cried. "Do let me keep it. It seems just a bit of home—a bit of home—a bit of home."

He murmured it over and over again, as if there was rest and happiness in the very sound of it.

"I'll keep fresh as long as ever I can," said the pansy, "It's the least I can do for him, poor fellow!"

"At all events the flowers are all out of my own garden," said Bethea, sitting down by the white bed, and then she talked away so gently that the boy's weary face smoothed out, and he went to sleep.

In a few days' time Bethea begged her grandmother to let

her go again to the hospital, and she persuaded the gardener
to give her a beautiful bunch of pansies to take to the
sick boy.

As she entered the room, she saw that the little purple
pansy was standing in a tumbler of water, on a chair by the
boy's bed.

Its head hung over on one side, but it looked quite fresh
and healthy.

" Hasn't it lasted well ? " said the boy, happily. He looked
much better and spoke in a loud, cheerful voice. " It's been
talking to me about all sorts of things ! the country, and
gardens, and springtime, and being out and about in the
fresh air and sunshine ! "

" Well, I certainly have tried to make myself as pleasant
as possible," said the pansy, but it spoke so low that nobody
heard it except the boy whose ears were sharpened by illness.

" I've brought you some more," said Bethea, holding out
her bouquet, " shall I put them in the tumbler with the
little one ? "

" Oh, no ! " cried the boy anxiously, " I think if you don't
mind I'd rather you gave those to some of the other children.
I can't like any fine new flowers as well as that little fellow.
I feel as if he had made me well again ! "

The pansy expanded with pride, and a tear of gratitude
rolled out of its eye, and fell with a splash on the cane
chair-seat.

" I'm going to have it dried in my old pocket book, when

it's really withered," continued the boy, "and then I shall be able to look at it always."

When little Bethea next visited the hospital, the boy with the crooked leg was just leaving; but his leg was not crooked any longer; his face was bright and healthy, and safely buttoned up in his coat he carried a shabby old pocket book, in which lay a withered flower, with one word written underneath in large pencilled letters—"*Heartsease.*"

A Story of Siena.

CHAPTER I.

THE house stands on a hill on the outskirts of Siena, not far from the high red walls that still enclose the town, as entirely as they did in the times long passed by, when Siena was the powerful rival of Florence.

Old frescoes, and the stone coats-of-arms of the dead and gone rulers of the place, decorate the great gates; which seem only waiting for a troop of knights and soldiers to pass through, and with a blast of their bugles awake the ancient inhabitants of the crooked streets, and fill them once more with the picturesque crowds of the middle ages.

We can imagine that the old owners are but lying asleep in their many storied gothic palaces, their vaulted courtyards, and shady loggias; ready to rub their eyes and come out as they hear the well-known sounds ringing across the wide piazza.

But the knights never come, and the old people go on sleeping; and the new people walk about the streets, and haggle at the market, and drive their country carts with the great patient white oxen, and crowd on Sunday up the broad

Cathedral steps to kneel in the dim light before the lighted altar, as generations have done before them.

All round the town stretches the open country. Low sandy hills dotted with olive and cyprus trees, melting into a blue sweep of mountains; and about a mile from one of the gates stands the rambling white house with closed shutters in which Maddalena, the housekeeper, lived alone with her two grand-children.

She was a kind old woman and fond of the twins, who had been left orphans when they were mere babies, but she often thought that surely no grandmother had ever been plagued before, as she was plagued by Tuttu and Tutti.

" When they were infants it was easy enough," she would declare to a sympathizing neighbour. " Give them a fig or something to play with, and they were perfectly happy; but at times now I am tempted to wish they had no legs, what with accidents and mischief.—Not that they're not fine children, and may be a comfort to my old age, but it's a harassing thing, waiting."

It was certainly a fact that Tuttu and Tutti were constantly in mischief; and yet their curly black heads, red cheeks, and great brown eyes, were so attractive, that people—even those whose property had been seriously injured by them—treated them leniently, and let them off with a scolding.

The twins were always repentant after one of their misfortunes, and made serious promises of amendment; but at the next temptation they forgot all their good resolutions, and never remembered them until they were in disgrace again.

Grandmother Maddalena devised numerous punishments for the children, such as tacking a cow's head cut out of red stuff, on their backs, when they had teazed Aunt Eucilda's cow—or tieing them up by one leg, with a long cord to the table, for stone-throwing; but Tutto and Tutti were incorrigible.

They wept loudly, embraced their grandmother, made all kinds of promises—and the next day went off to do just the same things all over again.

There was only one person who had any influence over them, Father Giacomo, the priest of the little Church of Sancta Maria del Fiore, close by. He had known them from the time they were helpless babies in swaddling clothes, till they grew to be mischievous creatures in homespun trousers; and in every stage of character and clothing he had borne with them, taught them, played with them, and loved them, until the *Padre* had become their idea of all that was wise and good, and they would do more for the sake of pleasing him than for anyone in the world, not even excepting their grandmother.

Every Sunday afternoon Father Giacomo called to take them for a walk, the one only sure way of keeping them out of mischief; and sometimes to their great delight they would go along the olive-bordered road to Siena, returning in the evening to the *Padre's* house, in time to have a good game with the two cats Neri and Bianca, who had lived there since their infancy, as important members of the household.

On their eighth birthday, Tuttu and Tutti assured their grandmother that they really intended to reform. They promised faithfully to give up tree climbing, fishing in the pond, and many other favourite sports, and commenced to dig in the piece of kitchen garden under their grandmother's direction. In fact so zealous did Tuttu become that he borrowed a knife from one of the farm labourers who was vine pruning, and cut the whole of the branches off a vine near the house, ending with a terrible gash in his own thumb, which necessitated his being carried in an ox-cart to the hospital in Siena, supported in his grandmother's arms; while Tutti walked behind weeping bitterly, under the impression that the doctor would certainly kill Tuttu this time for his carelessness.

Tuttu was not killed, however. The cut was sewn up, while the ox-cart with its good-natured driver waited outside, and the depressed party returned home, grandmother Maddalena clasping her little earthen pot full of hot wood ashes, which even in the excitement of the accident she had not forgotten to take with her, for it was a cold day in early spring-time.*

Tutti was allowed to ride home in the cart, and sat holding Tuttu's hand, his eyes round with solemnity, the traces of tears still on his cheeks.

* A *scaldino*, carried about by all the Siennese women, and used in the house instead of a fire.

That night he went to sleep with his arm thrown round Tuttu's neck, his curly head resting against his shoulder— and though Tuttu was cramped and uncomfortable, and his thumb pained him, he remained heroically still until he also dropped asleep, and the two little brothers dreamed peacefully of pleasant things until the morning.

CHAPTER II.

" Well, thank Heaven ! those children are safe for the present," said Maddalena, as she sat on a stone bench in the sun, with the dark clipped cyprus hedge behind her.

To the right rose the stuccoed *Palazzo*, with its great stone coat-of-arms hanging over the entrance, and inside, a peep of the shady courtyard, with green tubs of orange trees, and the twinkle of a fountain that shot up high into the sunshine, and fell with a splash into a marble basin.

Maddalena, in her broad Tuscan hat with its old-fashioned black velvet—for she would never give in to the modern innovations of flowers and ostrich feathers—held her distaff in her hand, and as she twisted the spindle and drew out the thread evenly, she thought with satisfaction of the improved behaviour of the twins.

Ever since the accident they had been different creatures, and she wondered how long it would be before they could be apprenticed to some useful trade, and begin to bring in a little money.

" When I can get hold of the Padre alone I'll ask him
about it; but he really does spoil these boys till I don't
know which tyrannizes over him most—the two cats or the
two children ! "

Maddalena's reflections were suddenly interrupted at this
point by the appearance of her grandchildren from the back
of the yew hedge by which she was sitting—Tuttu on all
fours, neighing like a horse, with Tutti on his back, blowing
a clay whistle.

" We're only doing ' cavalry,' grandmother," gasped
Tuttu, with a scarlet face, attempting to prance in a
military manner.

" Cavalry ! " cried Maddalena, starting up. " Those
children will be the death of me. Cavalry indeed ! Look
at your trousers, you disgrace. All the knees yellow sand,
and the elbows in holes ! " and she seized her distaff and
waved it at them threateningly.

To avoid his grandmother's arm, Tuttu hastily scrambled
under the stone seat, but his unfortunate rider thrown off
his balance, fell head first against the earthen *scaldino*, which
was broken, and its ashes scattered on the path in all
directions.

When Tuttu, lying flat with only his head visible, saw this
terrible misfortune ; he crawled out from his hiding-place,
and taking Tutti's hand helped him to get up, and stood
courageously in front of his grandmother.

" It was all my fault, grandmother. Don't scold him ! I

made him do it, and I'm so sorry," he said, with a quiver in his voice, but Maddalena was too angry to listen to him. She had thrown her distaff on the ground, and was picking up the pieces of the yellow *scaldino* to see if it could possibly be fitted together again.

"Go in both of you to bed," she called out without looking up, "and don't let me see either of you again to-day! Just when I had a moment's peace too, thinking you were at the Padre's. It really is too much."

Tutti burst into loud sobs of terror and remorse, but Tuttu took him by the hand and, without speaking, led him away to the house.

"Why don't you cry, too, Tuttu?" asked Tutti, stopping his tears to look in astonishment at his brother.

"I'm too old," said Tuttu. "Grandmother's quite right, we do behave badly to her." And that was the beginning of a new era for Tuttu.

The next day as soon as he was awake, he began to think seriously over any possible way by which he could earn enough money to buy a new *scaldino*. He dressed hurriedly and ran off to talk it over with Father Giacomo, and the result of the conference was a long but kind lecture of good advice, and permission to weed in the Padre's garden for the sum of one halfpenny for a large basketful.

Tuttu danced about with delight. "Why, I shall earn the money in no time at that rate," he cried, "and I'll buy the best *scaldino* in Siena!"

C

He felt that he must commence work immediately, and in the evening he staggered into Father Giacomo's, with a scarlet face, carrying a great hamper of green stuff.

When he had a little recovered himself, he unfolded to his old friend another plan he had thought of during the day, which he was quite sure would please his grandmother.

" I've got a broken *fiasco* that the gardener's given me," he said, "and I and Tutti mean to put a bean each into it every day we are really good. Then, at the end of the month—a whole month, mind!—we might take it up to grandmother."

Father Giacomo highly approved of this idea, and encouraged the children by every means in his power ; so that, for more than three weeks, the beans went in regularly and the halfpence in Tuttu's store, which he kept like a magpie hidden away in a crack of the woodwork, increased rapidly.

Old Maddalena had long ago forgiven the children, for though she was often angry with them, she loved them really. She guessed that Tuttu was determined to replace the *scaldino*, as on several occasions he had not been able to resist a veiled hint on the subject ; but she pretended perfect ignorance, and the two little boys might whisper and laugh to their heart's content—it was quite certain she never heard anything !

One soft evening in May, Tuttu came into the Palazzo garden in a state of great excitement. His last basket of weeds had been handed in to Father Giacomo, and the entire sum for the *scaldino* lay in small copper pieces in a crumpled scarlet pocket handkerchief.

"It's all here," whispered Tuttu, one great smile stretching across his good-tempered little face. "Every penny of it!— Shall it be brown or yellow? It must have a pattern. We'll go into Siena to-morrow and buy it."

"To Siena!" said Tutti in an awe-struck whisper, "We've never been there by ourselves."

"Never mind, we're older now," replied Tuttu. "Don't you say anything about it, it's to be a surprise from beginning to end."

Tutti agreed, as he always did with his brother. Of course Tuttu knew best, and it would sure to be all right.

CHAPTER III.

They started early in the morning, having put on their holiday clothes and brushed themselves; and as Bianca, who had come over from the Padre's house, insisted on following them, they tied a string to her red collar and determined to let her share the pleasure of their visit to the "great town."

Their grandmother was still sleeping, but they left word with the gardener's boy that they had gone into Siena "on business."

This sounded well, Tuttu thought, and would disarm suspicion.

The walk along the dusty high road was long and tiring, and they were glad when they arrived safely in the Piazza, where the market people had already begun to collect, for it was market day.

Tuttu carried his precious earnings tied up with intricate knots in the handkerchief, and stowed away in the largest of his pockets. He walked with conscious pride, knowing that he was a person of "property," and entering the pottery shop at the corner of the Piazza, began to cunningly tap the *scaldinos*, and peer into them; while Tutti stood by, lost in admiration at his brother's acuteness.

Finally, a brown pot, with yellow stripes and spots, was chosen and paid for, wrapped in the red handkerchief, and carried off in triumph towards the Porta Camolla.

"Whatever will grandmother say!" cried Tuttu, almost shouting for joy, "I wish I could run all the way. There'll be a big bean in the *fiasco* for each of us to-night, won't there, Tutti?"

"You've got a little money left, haven't you, Tuttu?" enquired Tutti, who was always practical; "Couldn't we buy some cakes. I really feel very hungry."

"Certainly not," said Tuttu, firmly, "I shall put it inside the *scaldino* for grandmother. That'll be the second surprise. Don't you see, Tutti?"

"But it's only two half-pennies," argued Tutti.

" Oh, she'll be glad enough of that!" said Tuttu, and tramped on steadily up the street. "Come along, Tutti, we'll go into the Cathedral."

Tutti remonstrated no more, he knew it was useless; and the two little boys, ascending a steep flight of steps, entered the Cathedral at a side door, and knelt down in the dim light in one of the chapels.

Tuttu repeated a prayer he had been taught, and then continued rapidly, "Thank you, too, very much, for making me and Tutti good; and please let us go on putting beans into the *fiasco* till it can't hold any more— and then we'll find something else . . . ." He paused to meditate. " Make grandmother pleased with us, and bless the cats."

Here Tuttu could think of nothing else, and nudged Tutti.

" You go on, Tutti."

" I think Tuttu's said everything," commenced Tutti in a whisper. " But please keep us out of the pond, and make us grow so that we can be artillery; and take us home safe, for the road's rather long, and we've never been there alone, and there's oxen about."

" You shouldn't say that, Tutti," said Tuttu, reprovingly. " Oxen won't hurt you, and you shouldn't be a coward."

" Well, shall I pray not to be a coward?" enquired Tutti.

" If you think it's necessary," said Tuttu. " But you can save that for another time—we ought to be going now"— so Tutti got up, and the children pushed their way through the heavy curtain by the door, and found themselves once more in the bright sunshine.

Certainly Bianca had been no trouble to them. In the Cathedral she behaved in the most serious manner, sitting by their side, and never moving until they pulled the string to which she was fastened; when she got up solemnly, and followed them on to the Piazza.

"I'm glad I prayed for you, Bianca, good cat!" said Tuttu. "You would never have allowed anyone to touch that *scaldino*, would you?"

Bianca mewed. She was rather bewildered by her walk through the town, but as long as her two friends were satisfied, that was enough for her.

As they came out upon the more crowded thoroughfare, the twins with their white cat attracted some attention, and many laughing remarks were shouted to them as they edged their way along the narrow paved street, where the absence of any pathway made it necessary to keep their eyes very wide open indeed, to avoid being run over by the carts and carriages.

Tutti walked in charge of Bianca, while Tuttu devoted all his attention to the *scaldino* in its red handkerchief, and a large green cotton umbrella he had brought from home in case the day should turn out to be rainy.

This umbrella seemed to be endowed with life, so extraordinary was its power of wriggling itself under the legs of the passers by. It had to be constantly wrenched out, with

many apologies, by its owner ; while the person who had been
nearly tripped up by it, went on his—or her—way grumbling.

No one did more than grumble, however, for the look of
horror on Tuttu's face was irresistible.

"THE TWINS WITH THEIR WHITE CAT ATTRACTED SOME ATTENTION."

"Go on, Tutti; do hurry!" he cried, urgently. "I'm
getting so hot with this horrible umbrella. It seems to
catch hold of people whichever way I carry it!"

" I *am* going," replied Tutti laconically.   " But remember,
I've got the cat."

As he spoke a boy darted out from one of the grim old
houses close by, and picking up a loose stone threw it at
Bianca, grazing her head, and leaving a great red stain that
commenced to trickle slowly down her spotless white body.

Tuttu, his eyes blazing with wrath, placed the *scaldino* by
the side of the kerbstone, and darted at the boy, waving his
umbrella ; while Tutti threw his arms round Bianca's neck
and tried to hush her mews of terror by a shower of tears
and kisses.

" How *dare* you ?" shouted Tuttu, beside himself with
anger. " Go away, and leave our poor Bianca ! You've
killed her, I expect ; and I wish I could kill you !"   But
even in the midst of his ungovernable rage, Tutti's voice
reached him.

" Oh, Tuttu, Tuttu ! the *scaldino !*"

Tuttu darted across the street towards the stone where
he had left the precious red bundle.   There it was, lying unhurt, and he was about to seize it and carry it to a place of
safety, when a fast-trotting horse with one of the light
country gigs behind him, dashed down the street.

" Get out of the way !   Get out of the way !" shouted the
driver—but it was too late !

The gig flew on, and Tuttu lay white and quiet, the
scaldino still grasped in his two little outstretched hands.

CHAPTER IV.

" Where's the *scaldino*, grandmother ? " were Tuttu's first words, when he woke up to find himself lying on a little bed in a long room, with Maddalena and Father Giacomo bending over him. " We saved up . . . It's all for you . . ." he muttered brokenly, " Have you got it ? "

" Yes, my lamb. A beautiful one it is," said the old woman, the tears streaming down her wrinkled face. " You lie still and get better, my Tuttu."

" I will, grandmother, but I want you to see the surprise inside. It's from weeding . . . Father Giacomo will tell you. I'm so tired, grandmother . . . . How's Bianca ? "

" Very well, Tuttu, she has only a slight scratch . . . Oh, my poor boy ! " and Father Giacomo's voice broke.

" Is it near evening ? " said Tuttu, after a few minutes, during which he lay moving his head restlessly.

" It soon will be," said the Padre. " Why do you ask, Tuttu ? "

" The *fiasco*. . . . Do you think I may put a bean in to-night, or was I too angry ? "

" You may, Tuttu," said Father Giacomo, turning away his head. " If you tell me where it is, I will send for it."

" By the melon bed. Tutti knows. He'll bring it," whispered Tuttu. " It's nearly full—only four days more. Put one in for Tutti."

As the setting sun streamed into the long room, Tutti

crept in, holding Father Giacomo's hand; carrying the broken *fiasco*.

Tuttu awoke from a restless sleep as they entered, and smiled with a faint reflection of his old happy laugh. "That's right, Tutti. You *have* been good, haven't you?"

"Yes," quavered Tutti, lifting his terrified, tear-stained face to his brother.

"Put your bean in then, Tutti, and give me mine. It's getting so late, it's almost night-time."

Tutti held out the bean with a trembling hand, and as it dropped into the old bottle, little Tuttu gave a quiet sigh.

"It only wants four more," he said happily.

Only four more! But Tuttu might never put them in. That night he started on a long, long journey, and as the old grandmother with choking sobs placed the broken bottle on a shelf among her treasures, she turned to Tutti who was lying, worn out with grief, upon the doorstep.

"Come, my Tutti," she said, "there are only us two now. We must try and be very good to each other."

     *   *   *   *   *   *

Years afterwards, Tutti, coming home on leave—for he had clung to his childish idea of being a soldier—found the broken *fiasco* in the corner where his grandmother had hidden it; and taking out the beans that had been lying there so long, he carried them to a little grave with a small white cross at the head of it.

"Dear Tuttu! He would like to have these growing round him," he thought, and planted them carefully amongst the flowers and grasses.

Grandmother Maddalena was too old to move out of the house now, but Father Giacomo watered the beans lovingly, and in the soft spring air they grew rapidly, so that they soon formed a beautiful tangle, hiding the cross and even the name that still stood there clearly in black letters

" TUTTU."

The Stone-Maiden.

ATVEN was the son of a fisherman, and lived with his father on a flat sandy coast far away in the North-land.

Great rocks strewed the shore about their hut, and the child had often been told how, long, long ago, the giant Thor fought single-handed against a shipload of wild men who attempted to land in the little bay; and drove them off—killing some, and changing others into the wonderful stones that remained there to that day.

The country people called them "Thor's balls;" and Atven often wandered about amongst them, trying to find likenesses to the old warriors in their weather-worn surfaces; and peering into every hole and cranny—half dreading, half hoping to see a stone hand stretched out to him from the misty shadows of the past.

Here and there, a row of smaller boulders lay half sunk in the sand, with only their rounded tops, covered with long brown seaweed, appearing above the surface.

These, Atven decided, must be the heads of the ancient Norsemen, and further on stood their huge mis-shapen bodies, twisted into every imaginable form, and covered by myriads of shell-fish, that clung to their grey sides like suits of shining armour.

Atven was often lonely; for he had no brothers or sisters, and his mother had died many years before. He was a shy, wild boy—more at home with the sea birds that flew about the lonely shore, than with the children he met sometimes as he wandered about the country; but in spite of his shyness he had friends who loved him everywhere he went. The house dogs on every farm knew his step, and ran out to greet him; the horses rubbed their noses softly upon his homespun tunic; the birds clustered on his shoulders; the cats came purring up, and the oxen lowed and shook their bells as soon as they caught sight of him. The very hens cackled loudly for joy—and Atven would caress them all with his brown hand, and had a kind word for every one of them.

All the short Northern summer, Atven spent his evenings in searching about amongst " Thor's balls " for traces of the warriors of the old legend; and one night, in the soft clearness of the twilight, he came upon something that rewarded him for all his patient perseverance.

Lifting a mass of seaweed that had completely covered one of the larger rocks, he saw before him the graceful form of a little Stone-maiden!

There she lay, as though quietly sleeping, her long dress falling in straight folds to her feet, her rippled hair spreading about her. One small hand grasped a chain upon her neck, the other was embedded in the rock on which she was lying.

Atven was so astonished that he stared at the child-figure as if turned into a statue himself.

Then he realized that his long search had been rewarded, and he fell on his knees and prayed that the Stone-maiden might be released from her prison, and given to him to be a little playfellow.

As soon as it was daylight the next morning, he started off to ask the advice of his one friend, the old Priest of Adgard.

The day was fine, with a crisp northern air, and a bright sun that danced on the long stretches of sandy grass, and on the swaying boughs of the fir trees.

Atven's heart beat hopefully as he neared the neat wooden house in which the old Priest lived.

Father Johannes welcomed him kindly, as he always did ; and listened attentively whilst Atven told his story.

" It must have consideration, my child," he said. " I will come down to the shore to-morrow—perhaps I may be able to think of something."

Atven took up his cap humbly, and started on his home-ward journey.

As he threaded his way beneath the shadows of the pine-trees, the sun's fingers darted through the branches and drew a golden pattern on the mossy ground under his feet ; the mosquitoes hummed drowsily, the air was full of soft summer warmth and brightness—but Atven's thoughts were far away with the ancient legend and the Stone-maiden.

How had she come to be amongst the shipload of "wild-men" in the misty ages when Thor yet walked the earth? Had she a father and mother who loved her, and perhaps brothers and sisters—and how long had she been sleeping so quietly in the arms of the great rock?

It was a strange cradle, with only the sea to sing her lullaby, and wash her lovingly, like a tender mother!

Atven hurried on; and as he peered before him with sun-dazzled eyes, he thought he saw a figure flitting in and out between the brown tree stems.

It was a small, light figure, with a strange kind of loose dress, and long floating hair of a beautiful gold colour. It glided along so rapidly that Atven had some difficulty in keeping pace with it.

Every now and again it seemed to be beckoning to him with one little hand; and at last as he ran faster and faster, it suddenly turned its head, and he saw the face of a beautiful young woman. Her brown eyes were soft and clear, and her cheeks tinted with a colour so delicate, it reminded Atven of the little pink shells he sometimes found after a storm upon the sea-shore.

"Atven! Atven!" she murmured, "You have found my child. Give her life! Give her life!"

"Tell me what I am to do!" cried Atven, and stretched out his hands towards the beautiful young woman; but at that moment she reached the shore, and gliding between the boulders, disappeared amongst their dark shadows.

Atven threw himself down beside the rock on which the Stone-maiden lay sleeping. He grieved for her so much that tears rolled slowly down his cheeks, and as they touched the stone, the great boulder shook and crumbled, and a shudder passed over the figure of the Stone-maiden. She seemed to Atven to sigh gently, and half open her eyes; but in a moment they closed again; the rock settled into its place, and everything was motionless.

" To-morrow! To-morrow!" he said to himself, " When Father Johannes comes, he will help me."

Early next morning the old Priest knocked at the door of the fisherman's hut. He had started at daybreak, for he knew that Atven would be anxiously awaiting him.

They went down together to the shore; and when Father Johannes saw the figure of the sleeping child, he took out of his bark basket, a little jar of water from the Church Well, and sprinkled it over her.

The Stone-maiden stirred and opened her eyes. She raised her hands, breathed gently, and lifting her head, gazed at the old Priest and the boy with wistful brown eyes, like those of the figure Atven had met in the forest.

" Where is my father? Where am I ? " she asked, in a low soft voice, as she rose up from the rock, and shook out the folds of her long dress.

Father Johannes took her hand, and gently repeated the

old legend; while the Stone-maiden listened with wide-open eyes.

"I remember it all now," she said, as the puzzled look faded from her face. "We had but just landed when the thick cloud came down, and a shower of stones fell upon us. My father was smitten down with all his followers, and I only was left weeping upon the shore. A cold air seemed to breathe upon me, and I fell asleep."

She spoke slowly, in the old Norse tongue, but Father Johannes had studied it, and understood her without much questioning.

"Where was your mother?" he asked kindly, as Atven with smiles of delight, seized her other hand.

"My mother died just before we set sail, and my father would not leave me lonely," answered the Stone-maiden sadly.

"But we will all love you now," cried Atven. "I will grow tall and strong to work for you, and you shall never be unhappy any more!"

The Stone-maiden smiled, as she stood on the threshold of her new life. She looked up trustingly at her two friends, and the old Priest of Asgard, bending down, laid his hand upon her head with a gentle blessing.

*   *   *   *   *   *

The Warriors' heads, with their tangled elf-locks, still peer out of the drifting sand—the twisted bodies in their sea-

D

armour, lie half surrounded by the green waters; but the
log hut, and Atven have vanished into the misty shadows of
the past.   They, and the good old priest, have drifted away
to Shadow-Land.

Only the sea talks of them still; and croons them a lullaby,
as soft as the centuries-old song, it sang over the cradle of
the enchanted Stone-maiden.

The Grass of Parnassus.

O N the banks of a clear stream in one of the far away Greek islands, grew a small flowering plant, with delicate stem and transparent white flower, called "Grass of Parnassus."

Every day it saw its own face, reflected in the running water, and every day it made the same complaint—

"This place is beautiful, the soft earth wraps me round, the branches bend over me, but I can never be happy, for I have never seen a River-God!"

The fish swimming close to the shore had talked to the Grass, of the mysterious race who lived in the shallows of the river, higher up, where it broadened into a lake; and played on their rude pipes as they rested in the flickering gloom of the water-weeds and rushes.

"Everyone has seen the River-Gods but me!" said the white flower. "The wind brings me the floating sound of their piping—I can even hear their laughter, and the echo of their voices. Yet they do not come, and I may wither, and never have the happiness I long for!"

But one day, the river-side thrilled, with a strange, new

feeling of hope and expectation. The sun shone, a faint breeze stirred the trees; and down the stream waded a beautiful youth, carrying his pipes in his hand, blowing a few notes mournfully, at long intervals. His hair, crowned with an ivy wreath, hung down, curled and tangled; his hoof-feet splashed in the shallows of the water, and he cried—

"Nadiä! Nadiä! Where are you hiding—Why do you not come to me?"

The white flower remained, enchanted and motionless, upon its stem, bending its yellow eye upon the stranger.

"Nadiä! Nadiä!" the voice wailed, "Do not hide from me any more!—Come to me!"

The bushes rustled and parted; a delicate girl's face looked out, and a wood nymph in floating garments, slid to the side of the stream, and dabbled her white feet in the water.

The youth gave a cry of joy; "I have found you, Nadiä! I have piped to you, and called to you till I was weary; but I loved you, and at last I have found you!"

The wood nymph smiled as she sat in the flickering shadows—and the River-God bending down, gathered the Grass of Parnassus, and placed it timidly in her shining tresses.

The wish of the white flower had been fulfilled; but the end of its life's longing was—Death.

The Hedgehogs' Coffee Party.

A STORY OF THURINGIA.

CHAPTER I.

IT was winter time, and the Thuringia-Wald lay still and white under its snowy covering.

The fir trees waved their branches in the frosty air, and a clear moon had risen over the mountains.

All was quiet and deserted, except that a faint sound of music and singing floated on the wind, coming undoubtedly from the comfortable burrow of the Hedgehog family, who lived under one of the largest pine stumps.

Councillor Igel—for the father was a member of the Hedgehog Government—had consented to allow the young people to have one or two friends to coffee, and they had been dancing with the greatest spirit for the last half hour.

By the porcelain stove stood the Councillor's only brother, Uncle Columbus, who had devoted himself since childhood to learned pursuits, and was much respected by the rest of the family.

He looked down upon all amusements as frivolous, but

then he had been to College, so his superior mind was only what was to be expected.

The Councillor belonged to an ancient Thuringian race who had been settled for centuries in the forest near the little town of Ruhla. They were a proud family, for one of their uncles had, some years before, been called to take up the position of Court Hedgehog at the Royal country Palace, where he moved in the highest society, and occasionally invited his relations to visit him.

" But fifty miles is really almost too far to go with nothing but a cup of coffee at the end," said the Hedgehog-mother, "and he never invites us to sleep. We don't, therefore, see so much of him as we otherwise should do."

" That must be very trying," replied the Mole-mother, to whom these confidences were being poured out.

" Yes, for of course it would be an inestimable advantage to the children to see a little Court life. However, with the fashions altering so quickly, it would be difficult for me to arrange their dresses in the last mode—and I couldn't have them looked down upon."

" Of course not," humbly replied the Mole-mother. She was sitting by the table, with her homespun knitting in her hand; and though she was trying to pay attention to her friend's words, she was arranging her dinner for the next day at the same time, and wondering whether her eldest child could have one more tuck let out of her frock before Christmas time.

" It's all very well for the Hedgehog-mother," she thought. " She comes of a high family, and can live in luxury; but with all my children, and my poor husband working away from morning till night, I'm obliged to plan every coffee bean, or I could never keep the house together!"

The Councillor's wife, however, talked on without noticing her distraction.

" Do you ever find any inconveniences from living so near the town?" she enquired. " Do the boys ever annoy you? They are sometimes very ill-bred."

" Our house is in such a retired position, I seldom see any-one," replied the Mole-mother. " The Forester's family are our nearest neighbours, and really they are so kind they might almost be Moles themselves."

" That is very pleasant for you," said the Frau Councillor. " Our case is quite different. The Rats who keep the inn at the cross roads, are most disagreeable people. We can't associate with them."

" Gypsies!" cried Uncle Columbus at this moment. He had an unpleasant habit when he did not like the conversation, of suddenly reminding the family of a tragedy that had happened some sixty years ago, when a promising young Hedgehog had been carried off to captivity by a band of travelling Tinkers, and finally disposed of in a way too terrible to be alluded to.

The Councillor's wife looked angry, and hastily changed the subject.

"He is quite a trial to us sometimes!" she whispered to the Mole-mother. "Such bad taste to mention Gypsies. It makes me tremble in every quill!"

"I think I must be going now," said the Mole-mother hurriedly, putting away her knitting into a reticule, and tying a woollen hood over her head—for she felt that it would not do for strangers to be mixed up in these family matters.

Calling her children to her, she helped them into their warm galoshes; and lighting a small lantern, they were soon out in the snowy forest.

CHAPTER II.

"Oh, mother, I wish we were rich like the Hedgehogs," cried the eldest daughter, Emmie; "Wilhelm and Fritz are so fashionable, and on Berta's birthday they are going to give a grand coffee party, to which the Court Hedgehog is expected!"

"Well, they won't ask us, so you had better not think too much about it," said the Mole-mother; "don't let your mind run on vanities."

As she spoke they saw the two rats from the Inn coming towards them. The elder—the proprietor of the Inn—in a peasant's dress with a pipe in his mouth, dragging a small sledge on which three infant rats were seated, wrapped

"THE RATS WHO KEEP THE INN ARE MOST DISAGREEABLE PEOPLE."

in a fur rug, while their mother walked beside them, her homespun cloak trailing over the snow.

"Good evening, neighbours!" cried the Mole-mother pleasantly, for though she did not exactly approve of the Rat household, she always treated them with civility. "Where are you out so late? How well the children are looking!"

"Yes, they grow rapidly — bless their little tails and whiskers!" said the Rat-mother proudly. "We have just been to my brother's in the town, taking a cup of coffee with him, and there we heard some news. *I* can tell you! There's to be a grand Coffee Party at the Hedgehogs, and though all the guests have been invited, *we* alone are left out. Most insulting *I* call it!"

"Well, it *is* rude," allowed the Mole-mother, "but they've not asked us either. You see the Court Hedgehog is to be there, and so it is very select."

"Select! I'll make them select!" growled the proprietor of the Inn with a scowl. "Who are they I should like to know? They may have Gypsies upon them at any moment!"

"Oh, I hope not!" cried the Mole-mother.

"There's a Tinker's boy in the town," said the Innkeeper, darkly, "and he's always looking out for Hedgehogs—I shouldn't be surprised if he heard where the family live."

"Good-night!" said the Mole-mother, nervously, and hurried on with her children.

"Some mischief will be done if we don't watch," she said

to Emmie, who was a mole of unusual intelligence. " I'll tell your brother to keep his eye on the Rat Inn."

After about half an hour's walking, they arrived at home ; for their house was in a secluded position in the most un-frequented part of the forest.

Though very simple, it was clean and well kept, and furnished with a large cooking stove, a four-post bedstead, and a few wooden benches.

In the one arm-chair sat the Mole-father, reading the newspaper ; while his sister, Aunt Betta, with a cap with long streaming ribbons on her head, was busily stirring something in a saucepan.

As the Mole-mother and her family, descended the stone stairway that led from the upper air, a delicious smell of cooking greeted them. Two large tallow candles were burn-ing brightly, and altogether the house presented a very lively appearance.

" Here you are at last," cried the Mole-father. " Supper is just ready, and I have sent Karl to the Inn for some lager-beer."

" I wonder if he will hear anything," said the Mole-mother taking off her galoshes; and then she related all the news of the evening.

" If there isn't some mischief brewing, may I be made into waistcoats ! " exclaimed the Mole-father, throwing down his newspaper.

It was his favourite expression when much excited, and

never failed to give the Mole-mother a shiver all down her back. She called it such very strong language.

At this moment Karl came clattering down the steps.

"Oh, father! mother! I *have* heard something!" he shouted. "The Rat-father has started off to the Tinker's to tell the boy where the Hedgehogs are living!"

The Mole-mother sank down on a bench gasping.

"He's done it then! Oh, the poor Hedgehogs!" she cried wringing her hands, "They'll be cooked in clay before they can turn round."

"Don't be in such a hurry, wife," said the Mole-father. "I've thought of something. We won't terrify the Hedge-hogs—What can *they* do?—but we'll collect all the Moles of the neighbourhood, and make a burrow all round the house; then if the Tinker's son comes, he'll fall in, and can't get any further. What do you think of that, eh?"

"An excellent idea!" said the Mole-mother, recovering. "Send Karl round to-night, and begin the first thing to-morrow morning."

As soon as daylight dawned in the forest, the Mole-father, accompanied by his wife and children, and all their friends; went out in a long procession, with their shovels and wheelbarrows, and commenced work round the Hedgehogs' house.

The Councillor's family were so busily occupied in turning out, and arranging, their rooms for the festivity—which was to include a dance in the evening—that they had no time to take any notice of the Moles' digging; in fact they never even observed it. The younger Hedgehogs were roasting coffee. The house-mother sugared the cakes in the back-kitchen, while the Councillor, with a large holland apron, rubbed down the floor, and gave a final dust to the furniture.

As to Uncle Columbus—he sat on a sort of island of chairs in one corner, studying a book, and looking on misanthropically at the preparations.

The Moles, therefore, were quite uninterrupted, and burrowed away vigorously, until the earth all round the house was mined to a depth of several feet; and they returned home to dinner in high spirits.

"If that boy dares to venture, may I be made into waist-coats, if he doesn't fall in!" cried the Mole-father, wiping his face with a red cotton pocket-handkerchief—for though the snow was on the ground the work was exhausting.

CHAPTER III.

The Tinker's family sat round a fire, in one of the tumble-down wooden cottages that dotted the outskirts of the little town of Ruhla.

A small stove scarcely warmed the one room, for great cracks appeared in the walls in every direction.

"We've got no dinner to-day; are you going after those Hedgehogs?" said the Tinker to his son Otto. "Now you know where they are, it will be an easy thing to get hold of them."

"Yes; we'll have a fine supper to-night," said Otto, stamping his feet to get them warm. "Come with me, Johann, and we'll take the old sack over our shoulders to bring them back in."

They started off over the crisp snow sparkling in the early sunshine, away to the forest; and straight towards the great pine tree, which sheltered the underground home of Councillor Igel.

"Come, Johann!" cried Otto, bounding along over the slippery pathway; but Johann was small and fat, and his little legs could not keep pace with Otto's long ones. He soon fell behind, and Otto raced on by himself.

"Do be careful, Otto! There's lots of Moles here," cried little Johann, but Otto did not stop to listen. On he ran almost up to the pine tree; when Johann saw him suddenly jump into the air, and disappear through the snow with a loud shriek.

CHAPTER IV.

At the sound of the fall, the Councillor ran up the steps to his front door, and put out his head cautiously to see what was the matter.

"Gypsies!" said Uncle Columbus without raising his eyes

from his book ; and for the first time in his life he was right !

Gypsies it certainly was, as the Councillor soon determined ; and he hastily scratched some snow over the door,
and retired to the back kitchen with his whole family, in a
terrible state of fright and excitement.

" What *can* the boy have fallen into ? " he enquired vainly
of the Hedgehog-mother, and of Uncle Columbus, in turn.
" There are no houses there that *I* know of. We have been
saved by almost a miracle ! "

As they remained shuddering in a little frightened knot—
only Uncle Columbus maintaining his philosophical calm—
the air filled with the odour of burnt sugar ; a faint knocking
was heard against the side of the stove pipe, and in another
minute the Mole-father's red nightcap appeared through a
hole, and his kind face shortly followed.

" Don't be frightened," he said reassuringly. " I have
made a little tunnel and come through—merely to
explain things. I thought perhaps you might be a little
alarmed."

" Alarmed ! " cried the Hedgehog-mother. " It doesn't
describe it ! Terrified, and distracted, is nearer to the real
thing. The sugar biscuits are all spoilt, for I forgot them
in the oven ; and my daughter Berta fainted on the top of
the stove, and is so seriously singed, she will be unable to
appear at the party. Not that we shall be able to have a
party now," continued the Hedgehog-mother, weeping, " for
Uncle Columbus sat down on the plum cake in mistake for a

foot-stool, and Fritz has trodden on the punch bottles. Oh, what a series of misfortunes!"

"Cheer up, my good neighbour, all will come right in time," said the Mole-father encouragingly.

"As long as the Court Hedgehog doesn't appear in the middle," wailed the Councillor. " It makes me shudder in every quill to think of it. Not even a front door to receive him at!"

"Oh, as to that, let him come to us, and we will give him the best we have," replied the Mole-father. " Our place is homely, but I daresay he will condescend to put up with it till your house is in order again. I sent Karl on to intercept him, and explain just how it is. He will take him straight to our house till you are ready for him."

" Well, I must say you have been exceedingly thoughtful," said the Councillor, pompously, " and I feel sincerely grateful to you; but now, will you kindly explain to me the cause of this severe disturbance?"

" I think I'll come into the room first, if you'll allow me," said the Mole-father. "I am getting rather a crick in the neck from sticking my head through here."

"Come in by all means," said the Hedgehog-mother, graciously. "I am sorry to be obliged to receive you in this humble apartment."

"Gypsies!" growled Uncle Columbus, who was brushing the currants and crumbs off his coat with a duster.

The Mole-father had by this time worked himself into the

kitchen, dragging his spade after him ; and seated on a bench by the stove, he related the whole story to the Councillor, but carefully omitted to give the name of the person who had betrayed the Hedgehogs to the Tinker's family; and not-withstanding the requests of the whole family, he firmly refused to do so.

"All's well that ends well," he said cheerfully, "and as I heard the Tinker forbidding his sons ever to come near the place again, you will be quite safe in the future."

"What has happened to that dreadful boy? Is he still in the hole, or have they got him out?" enquired the Hedgehog-mother anxiously.

"Got him out some time ago," said the Mole-father, "and carried him off to the hospital. Broke his leg, I am sorry to say, though it's nothing very bad. He will be all right in six weeks or so. I don't think much of those human fractures."

"Serves him right," said the Councillor viciously. "And now, my good preserver, in what way can we show our gratitude to you? I shall send Fritz and Wilhelm into the town for more provisions, and we might have our Coffee Party after all. What do you say to that, my children?"

The family clapped their hands joyfully.

"I trust you and your family will grace the party?" said the Hedgehog-mother to the old Mole.

"On one condition," he replied, "I shall be delighted to do so ; and that is that you will allow me to ask the Rats

from the Inn. They are touchy people, and do not readily
forgive an injury."

"What I said all along," muttered Uncle Columbus,
lifting his eyes from his dusting. "I said 'away with pride,'
but I wasn't listened to."

"You will be now," said the Councillor in a soothing and
dignified manner. "Certainly; send an invitation to the
Inn if you wish it. Just write, 'To meet the Court Hedgehog,' at the top, Wilhelm; it will make it more gratifying."

CHAPTER V.

The Court Hedgehog, with an escort of six guards, had
meanwhile arrived at the Mole's house, and was being enter-
tained by the Mole-mother and her children, who were all
in a state of great nervousness.

The Court Hedgehog, however, appeared to be more
condescending than could have been expected from his
position. He accepted some refreshment, and a pipe of
the Mole-father's tobacco, and then reclining in the one
easy chair, he awaited the course of events with calmness.

Here the Councillor found him some hours later, when the
confusion in the Hedgehog household having been smoothed
over—a deputation of the father and sons started to bring
the distinguished guest home in triumph.

The rooms in the Councillor's house had all been gaily

E

decorated with pine branches; the stove sent out a pleasant glow; and the Hedgehog-mother, in her best cap and a stiff black silk dress, stood waiting to welcome her guests in the ante-room.

By her side sat Berta, who had fortunately recovered sufficiently to be present at the entertainment; though still suffering from the effects of the shock, and with her head tied up in a silk handkerchief.

As the Court Hedgehog appeared in the door-way, three of the younger children, concealed in a bower of branches, commenced to sing an ode composed by Uncle Columbus for the occasion, beginning

"Welcome to our honoured guest," —while a fiddler hired for the occasion accompanied it upon the violin, behind a red curtain.

The first visitors to arrive were the Moles; followed by the Rat family, who were filled with remorse when they received the invitation, at the thought of their treacherous behaviour.

"I declare, mother," said the Inn-keeper to his wife in a whisper, "the Mole-father is such a good creature, I shall be ashamed to quarrel with any of his friends for the future. ' Live and let live,' ought to be our motto."

Uncle Columbus did not appear till late in the evening, when he entered the room dressed in an antiquated blue coat with brass buttons, finished off by a high stand-up white collar.

He staggered in, carrying a large plum cake about twice the size of the one he had unfortunately sat down upon; which he placed upon the coffee table, where the Hedgehog-mother was presiding over a large collection of various cups, mugs, and saucers.

"I have only just come back from town, where I went to procure a cake fit for this happy occasion," he whispered. "It does my heart good to see this neighbourly gathering, and I have made up my mind to promise you something in memory of the event. I will from this day, give up for ever a habit which I know has been objectionable to you—the word ' Gypsies ' shall never again be mentioned in the family."

Uncle Volodia.

A Story of a Russian Village.

CHAPTER I.

N the one hill of the district, just outside the village of Viletna, stood the great house belonging to Madame Olsheffsky.

All round it lay, what had once in the days gone by, been elaborate gardens, but were now a mere tangle of brushwood, waving grass, and wild flowers.

Beyond this, again, were fields of rye and hemp, bounded on one side by the shining waters of the great Seloe Lake, dug by hundreds of slaves in the time of Madame Olsheffsky's great-grandfather; and on the other by the dim greenness of a pine forest, which stretched away into the distance for mile after mile, until it seemed to melt into the misty line of the horizon.

Between the lake and the gardens of the great house, lay Viletna, with its rough log houses, sandy street, and great Church, crowned with a cupola like a gaily-painted melon; where Elena, Boris, and Daria, the three children of Madame

Olsheffsky, drove every Sunday with their mother in the old-fashioned, tumble-down carriage.

All the week the children looked forward to this expedition, for with the exception of an occasional visit to Volodia Ivanovitch's shop in the village, it was the only break in the quiet monotony of their lives.

They were allowed to go to Volodia's, whenever they had money enough to buy anything ; and often spent the afternoon there listening to his long tales, and examining the contents of the shop, which seemed to supply all that any reasonable person could wish for—from a ball of twine to a wedding dress.

Volodia himself, had been a servant at the great house many years before, " when the place was kept up as a country gentleman's should be"—he was fond of explaining to the children—" but when the poor dear master was taken off to Siberia—he was as good as a saint, and no one knew what they found out against him—then the Government took all his money, and your mother had to manage as well as she could with the little property left her by your grandfather. She ought to have owned all the country round, but your great-grandfather was an extravagant man, Boris Andreïevitch ! and he sold everything he could lay hands on ! "

Elena and Boris always listened respectfully. They had the greatest opinion of " Uncle Volodia's" wisdom, and they could just remember the time of grief and excitement when their father left them ; but it had all happened so long ago that though their mother often spoke of him, and their old nurse Var-Vara was never tired of relating anecdotes of his childhood, they had gradually begun to think of him, not as a living person, but as one of the heroes of the old romances that still lingered on the shelves of the dilapidated library.

It was a happy life the children led in the great white house. It made no difference to them that the furniture was old and scanty, that the rooms were bare, and the plaster falling away in many places from the walls and ceilings.

Their mother was there, and all their old friends, and they wished for nothing further.

Was there not Toulu, the horse, in his stall in the ruined stable; Tulipan, the Pomeranian dog, Adam, the old butler, and Alexis, the " man of all work," who rowed their boat on the lake, tidied the garden—as well as the weeds and his own natural laziness would allow him—and was regarded by Boris as the type of all manly perfection !

What could children want more ? Especially as Volodia was always ready at a moment's notice to tell them a story, carve them a peasant or a dog from a chip of pine-wood, dance a jig, or entertain them in a hundred other ways dear to the heart of Russian children.

CHAPTER II.

On one of the clear dry days of an early Russian autumn, when a brilliant glow of colour and sunshine floods the air, and the birch trees turned to golden glories shake their fluttering leaves like brilliant butterflies, Elena, Boris, and Daria, stood on one of the wide balconies of the great house, with their mother beside them, sorting seeds and tying them up in packets for the spring-time.

Some large hydrangeas, and orange trees, in green tubs, made a background to the little scene.

The eager children with clumsy fingers, bent on being useful; the pale, thin mother leaning back in her garden chair smiling at their absorbed faces.

"Children, I have something I must tell you," commenced Madame Olsheffsky, seriously, when the last seeds had been put away and labelled. "It is something that will make you sad, but you must try and bear it well for my sake, and for your poor father's—who I hope will return to us one day. I think you are old enough to know something about our affairs, Elena, for you are nearly thirteen. Even my little Boris is almost eleven. Don't look so frightened, darling," continued Madame Olsheffsky, taking little Daria in her arms, "it is nothing very dreadful. I am obliged to enter into a lawsuit—a troublesome, difficult lawsuit. One of our distant cousins has just found some papers which he thinks will prove that he ought to have had this estate instead of your grandfather, and he is going to try and take it from us. I have sent a great box of our title deeds to the lawyer in Viletna, and he is to go through them immediately—but who knows how it may turn out? Oh, children! you must help me bravely, if more ill-fortune is to fall upon us!"

Elena rushed towards her mother, and threw her arms round her neck. "We will! We will! Don't trouble about it, dear little mother," she cried. "What does it matter if we are all together. *I* will work and dig in the garden, and Boris can be taught to groom Toulu, and be useful—he really can be very sensible if he likes. Then Var-Vara will cook, and Adam and Daria can do the dusting. Oh, we shall manage beautifully!"

Madame Olsheffsky smiled through some tears.

"You are a dear child, Elena! I won't complain any more while I have all my children to help me. But run now Boris, and tell Alexis to get the boat ready. I must go to the other side of the lake, to see that poor child who broke his arm the other day."

Boris ran off to the stables with alacrity. He found it difficult to realize all that his mother had just told them. "Of course it was very dreadful," he thought, "but very likely it wouldn't come true. Then, as Elena said, nothing mattered much if they were all together; and perhaps, if they were obliged to move into the village, they might live near Volodia's shop; and the wicked cousin might let them come and play sometimes in the garden."

"Alexis! Alexis!" he shouted into the hay loft, and a brown face with a shock of black hair, appeared at one of the windows.

"What is it, Boris Andreïevitch?"

"Mamma wants the boat immediately," replied Boris. "She is going over to see Marsha's sick child."

Alexis took a handful of sunflower seeds out of his pocket, and began to eat them meditatively, throwing the husks behind him.

"The mistress won't go another day?" he enquired slowly.

Boris shook his head.

"The lake's overflowing, and the dam is none too strong over there by Viletna," continued Alexis; "it would be better for her to wait a little."

"She says she must go to-day," said Boris, "but I will tell her what you say."

Madame Olsheffsky, however, refused to put off her visit; and Elena, Boris, and Daria, looking out from the balcony, saw the boat with the two figures in it start off from the little landing-place, and grow smaller and smaller, until it faded away into a dim speck in the distance.

CHAPTER III.

Late that afternoon the three children were playing with
Tulipan in the garden, when they heard Volodia's well-
known voice shouting to them—

"Elena! Boris Andreïevitch!"

They fancied he seemed to be in a great hurry, and as
they flew towards him, they noticed that he had no hat, and
there was a look of terror on his face that froze Elena's heart
with the certainty of some unknown but terrible misfortune.

"The lake! the lake!" he panted; "where is the mistress?"

"Gone to see Marsha's sick child," said Elena, clinging
to little Daria with one hand, and gazing at Volodia with
eyes full of terror.

"Ah, then it is true. It was her I saw! The poor
mistress! Aïe! Aïe! Don't move, children! Don't stir.
Here is your only safety," cried Volodia in piercing tones.
"The river has flooded into the lake, and the dam
may go any moment. The village will be overwhelmed.
Nothing can save it! The water rises! rises! and any
minute it may burst through! The Saints have mercy!
All our things will be lost; but it is the will of God—we
cannot fight against it." And Volodia crossed himself
devoutly with Russian fatalism.

"But mamma! what will happen to her?" cried Elena
passionately. "Can nothing be done?"

"To go towards the lake now would be certain death,"

replied Volodia brokenly. "No, Elena Andreïevna; we must trust in God. He alone can save her if she is on the water now! Pray Heaven she may not have started!"

As he spoke, a long procession of terrified peasants came winding up the road towards the great house. All the inhabitants of the village had fled from their threatened homes, and were taking refuge on the only hill in the neighbourhood.

Weeping, gesticulating and talking; the men, women, and children, rushed on in the greatest state of confusion.

Some carried a few possessions they had snatched up hastily as they left their houses, some helped the old bedridden people to hobble along on their sticks and crutches; others led the smaller children, or carried the gaily-painted chests containing the holiday clothes of the family; while the boys dragged along the rough unkempt horses, and the few cows and oxen they had been able to drive in from the fields close by.

All, as they came within speaking distance of Elena and Boris, began to describe their misfortunes ; and such a babel of sound rose on the air that it was impossible to separate one word from another.

" Where shall they go to, *Matoushka?*"* enquired Volodia anxiously, as the strange procession spread itself out amongst the low-growing birch trees.

Elena shook herself, as if awakening from a horrible dream.

---

* *Matoushka*—little mother.

"Oh, it is dreadful! dreadful! But you are welcome, poor
people!" she cried. " Put the horses into the stables—Adam
will show you where—and the dogs too ; and come into the
house all of you, if you can get in. The cows must go to
the yard. Oh, Var-Vara !" she added, as she turned to her
old nurse, who had just come out, attracted by the noise.
" Have you heard ? Oh, poor mamma ! Do you think she
will be safe ?" and Elena rushed into the house, and up the
stair of a wooden tower, from which she could see for miles
round, a wide vista of field, lake, and forest.

No boat was in sight, and the lake looked comparatively
peaceful ; but just across the middle stretched an ominous
streak of muddy, rushing water, that beat against the high
grass-grown dam, separating the lake from the village, and
threatened every moment to roll over it.

Elena held her breath, and listened. There was a dull
roaring sound like distant thunder.

The streak of brown water surged higher and higher ; and
suddenly—in one instant, as it seemed to the terrified child—
a vast volume of water shot over the dam, seeming to carry
it away bodily with its violence ; and with a crash like an
earthquake, the pent-up lake burst out in one huge wave, that
rolled towards the village of Viletna, tearing up everything it
passed upon its way.

Elena turned, and, almost falling downstairs in her terror,
ran headlong towards the group of peasants who had gathered
on the grass before the wooden verandah, and in despairing

silence were watching the destruction of their fields and houses.

Beside them stood the old Priest, his long white hair shining in the sunshine.

" My children, let us pray to the good God for any living things that are in danger ! " he said.

The peasants fell upon their knees.

" Save them! Save them ! " they cried, imploringly, " and save our cattle and houses ! "

The blue sky stretched overhead, all round the garden the birch trees shed their quivering glory; the very flowers that the three children had picked for their mother, in the morning, lay on a table fresh and unfaded; yet it seemed to Elena that years must have passed by since she stood there, careless and happy.

" Oh, Boris, come with me ! " she cried, passionately, " I can't bear it ! "

Boris, with the tears falling slowly from his eyes, followed his sister up to the tower, and there they remained till evening, straining their eyes over the wide stretch of desolate-looking water.

CHAPTER IV.

It was some months afterwards. The flood was over, and the people of Viletna had begun to rebuild their log houses, and collect what could be found of their scattered belongings.

A portion of the great dyke had remained standing, so that the lake did not completely empty itself; and the peasants were able, with some help from the Government, to rebuild it.

Everyone had suffered; but the heaviest blow had fallen upon the great house, for Madame Olsheffsky never returned to it. Her boat had been upset and carried away, with the sudden force of the current, and though Alexis managed to save himself by clinging to an uprooted pine tree, Madame Olsheffsky had been torn from him, and sucked under by the rush of the furious water.

Elena's face had grown pale and thin during these sad weeks, and she and Boris looked older; for they had begun to face the responsibilities of life, with no kind mother to stand between them and the hard reality.

To add to their misfortunes, the wooden box containing the title-deeds of their estate, and all their other valuable papers; had been swept away with the rest of Lawyer Drovnine's property, and there seemed no chance that it would ever be recovered again.

In the interval, as no defence was forthcoming, the lawsuit had been decided in favour of the Olsheffsky's cousin; and the children were now expecting every day to receive the notice that would turn them out of their old home, and leave them without a place in the world that really belonged to them.

The few relations they had, made no sign to show they knew of their existence ; but they were not without friends, and one of the first and truest of these was Volodia.

"Don't trouble about this law-suit, Elena Andreïevna," he said, on one of his frequent visits to the great house. "If the wickedness of the world is so great, that they rob you of what rightfully belongs to you; take no notice of it—it is the will of God. *You* will come down with Boris Andreïevitch, and Daria Andreïevna, to my house, where there is plenty of room for everyone ; and my wife will be proud and honoured. Then Var-Vara can live with her brother close by—a good honest man, who is well able to provide for her; and Adam will hire a little place, and retire with his savings. Alexis shall find a home for Toulu—You know Alexis works for his father on the farm now, and is really getting quite active. You see, *Matoushka*, every one is nicely provided for, and no one will suffer! "

" But how can we all live with you, when we have no money? " said Elena. "Good, kind Volodia! It would not be fair for us to be a burden to you! "

" How can you talk of burdens, Elena Andreïevna ! It's quite wrong of you, and really almost makes me angry! Your grandfather gave me all the money with which I started in life, and it's no more than paying back a little of it. Besides, think of the honour ! Think what a proud thing it will be for us. All the village will be envious ! "

Elena smiled sadly. "I suppose we shall have a little money left, shan't we, Volodia?"

"Of course, *Matoushka*. Plenty for everything you'll want."

And so, after much argument and discussion, with many tears and sad regrets, the three children said good-bye to the great house; and drove with Toulu down the hill for the last time, to Volodia's large new wooden house, which had been re-built in a far handsomer style than the log hut he had lived in formerly.

CHAPTER V.

Fortunately the winter that year was late in coming, so that the peasants of Viletna were able to build some sort of shelter for themselves before it set in with real severity.

Volodia's house, which stood in the centre of the village, had been finished long before any of his neighbours'.

"That's what comes of being a rich man," they said to each other, not grumbling, but stating a fact. "He can employ what men he likes; it is a fine thing to have money."

Volodia's shop had always been popular, but with the arrival of the three children it became ten times more so.

Everyone wished to show sympathy for their misfortunes; and all those who were sufficiently well off, brought a little present, and left it with Volodia's wife, with many mysterious nods and explanations.

"Don't tell *them* anything about it, but just cook it. It's a chicken we reared ourselves—one of those saved from the flood."

Volodia would have liked to give the things back again, but his wife declared this would be such an affront to the donors that she really couldn't undertake to do it.

"It's not for ourselves, Volodia Ivanovitch, but for those poor innocent children; I can't refuse what's kindly meant. Many's the *rouble* Anna Olsheffsky (of blessed memory) has given to the people here, and why shouldn't they be allowed to do their part?"

Meanwhile, Elena and Boris, were getting slowly used to their changed life. It still seemed more like a dream than a reality; but they began to feel at home in the wooden house, and Elena had even commenced to learn some needlework from Var-Vara, and to help Maria in as many ways as that active old woman would allow of.

"Don't you touch it, Elena Andreïevna," she would say, anxiously, "it's not fit you should work like us. Leave it to Adam, and Var-Vara, and me. We're used to it, and it's suitable."

And so Elena had to give herself up to being waited upon as tenderly by the old servants, as she had been during their time of happiness at the great house.

Boris had no time for brooding, for he was working hard at his lessons with the village Priest; and as to little Daria, she had quickly adapted herself to the new surroundings.

F

She played with Tulipan, made snow castles in Volodia's side yard, and whenever she had the chance, enjoyed a sledge drive with Alexis, in the forest.

" If only mamma were here, I should be quite happy," she said to Elena. "It does seem so dreadful, Elena, to think of that horrible flood. You don't think it will come again, do you ? "

Elena's eyes filled with tears, as she answered reassuringly.

"You'll see mamma some day, Daria, if you're a very good girl; and meantime, you know, she would like you to learn your lessons, and be as obedient as possible to Var-Vara."

" Well, I do try, Elena, but she *is* so tiresome sometimes. She won't let me play with the village children ! They're very nice, but she says they're peasants. I'm sure I try to remember what you teach me, though the things *are* so difficult. I'm not so *very* lazy, Elena ! "

Elena stooped her dark brown head over the little golden one.

" You're a darling, Daria ! I know you do your best, when you don't forget all about it ! "

Volodia Ivanovitch had devoted his two best rooms to the children. He had at first wished to give up the whole of his house to them, with the exception of one bedroom ; but Elena had developed a certain strength of character and resolution during their troubles, and absolutely refused to listen to this idea ; so that finally the old man was obliged to give way, and turn his attention to arranging the rooms, in a style of what he considered, surpassing elegance and comfort.

They were plain and simple, with fresh boarded walls and pine floors.

The furniture had all been brought from the great house, chosen by Volodia with very little idea of its suitability, but because of something in the colour or form that struck him as being particularly handsome.

A large gilt console table, with marble top, and looking glass, took up nearly one side of Elena's bedroom; and a glass chandelier hung from the centre of the ceiling—where it was always interfering with the heads of the unwary. The bed had faded blue satin hangings; and a large Turkish rug and two ricketty gilt chairs, completed an effect which Uncle Volodia and his wife considered to be truly magnificent.

Boris slept in the room adjoining.

This was turned into a sitting-room in the daytime, and furnished in the same luxurious manner. Chairs with enormous coats-of-arms, a vast Dresden china vase with a gilt cover to it; and in the corner a gold picture of a Saint with a little lamp before it, always kept burning night and day by the careful Var-Vara—Var-Vara in her bright red gold-bordered gown, and the strange tiara on her head, decorated with its long ribbons.

"If ever they wanted the help of the Saints, it's now," she would say, as she filled the glass bowl with oil, and hung it up by its chains again. "The wickedness of men has been too much for them. Aïe! Aïe! It's the Lord's will."

CHAPTER VI.

Volodia Ivanovitch's house stood close to the village street, so that as Elena looked from her windows she could see the long stretch of white road—the snow piled up in great walls on either side—the two rows of straggling, half-finished log huts, ending with the ruined Church, and the new posting-house.

In the distance, the flat surface of the frozen lake, the dark green of the pine forest, and the wide stretches of level country ; broken here and there by the tops of the scattered wooden fences.

Up the street the sledges ran evenly, the horses jangling the bells on their great arched collars, the drivers in their leather fur-lined coats, cracking their whips and shouting.

Now and then a woman, in a thick pelisse, a bright-coloured handkerchief on her head, would come by ; dragging a load of wood or carrying a child in her arms.

The air was stilly cold, with a sparkling clearness ; the sky as blue and brilliant as midsummer.

Elena felt cheered by the exhilarating brightness. She was young, and gradually she rose from the state of indifference into which she had fallen, and began to take her old interest in all that was going on about her.

"I want to ask you something, Uncle Volodia," she said one day, as they sat round the *samivar*,* for she had begged

* Tea-urn.

that they might have at least one meal together, in the sitting-room.

Maria was rather constrained on these occasions, seeming oppressed with the feeling that she must sit exactly in the centre of her chair. She spread a large clean handkerchief out over her knees, to catch any crumbs that might be wandering, and fixed her eyes on the children with respectful solemnity.

Volodia, on the contrary, always came in smiling genially, in his old homespun blouse and high boots ; and was ready for a game with Daria, or a romp with Boris, the moment the tea things had been carried away by his wife.

" What is it, Elena Andreïevna ? " he asked. " Nothing very serious, I hope ? "

" Not very, Uncle Volodia. It's only that I want to learn something—I want to feel I can *do* something when our money has gone, for I know it won't last very long."

" Why trouble your head about business, Elena Andreïevna ? You know your things sold for a great deal, and it is all put away in the wooden honey-box, in the clothes chest. It will last till you're an old woman ! "

" But I would like to *feel* I was earning some money, Uncle Volodia. I think I might learn to make paper flowers. Don't you think so, dear Uncle Volodia ? You know I began while mamma was with us ; the lady in Mourum taught me. I wish very much to go on with it."

Uncle Volodia pondered. It might be an amusement for

the poor girl, and no one need know of the crazy notion of selling them.

" If you like, *Matoushka*. Do just as you like," he said.

So it was decided that Elena should be driven over to Mourum on the next market day.

Volodia had undertaken, in the intervals of shop-keeping, to teach little Daria how to count ; with the elaborate arrangement of small coloured balls, on a wire frame like a gridiron, with which he added up his own sums—instead of pencil and paper.

They sat down side by side with the utmost gravity. Old Volodia with the frame in one hand, Daria on a low stool, her curly golden head bent forward over the balls, as she moved them up and down, with a pucker on her forehead.

" Two and one's five, and three's seven, and four's twelve, and six's —— "

"Oh, Daria Andreïevna ! You're not thinking about what you're doing ! "

" Oh, really I am, Uncle Volodia ; but those tiresome little yellow balls keep getting in the way."

And then the lesson began all over again, until Daria sprang up with a laugh, and shaking out her black frock, declared she had a pain in her neck, and must run about a little !

" What a child it is ! " cried Volodia admiringly. " If she lives to be a hundred, she'll never learn the multiplication table ! "

CHAPTER VII.

A post-sledge was gliding rapidly over the frozen road towards Viletna ; and as it neared the village, a thin worn man, with white hair, who was sitting in it alone, leant forward and touched the driver.

" I want to go to the great house. You remember ? "

" Oh, you're going to see Mikhail ? He hasn't come to the great house yet, though. It's all being done up."

" No, I'm going to Madame Olsheffsky's ! "

" Anna Olsheffsky ! Haven't you heard she was drowned in the flood ? Washed away. Just before the children lost their property to that thief of a cousin ! "

The driver went on adding the details, not noticing that the gentleman had fallen back, and lay gasping as if for air.

" You knew Anna Olsheffsky, perhaps ? " he said at last, turning towards the traveller. Then seeing his face, " Holy Saints ! What is the matter ? He'll die surely, and no help to be had ! "

" She was my wife," said the gentleman hoarsely. " You don't remember me ? I am André Olsheffsky."

"To think that I shouldn't have known you, *Barin !*" cried the driver in great excitement, dropping the reins. " Not that it's much to be wondered at, and you looking a young man when you left ! Welcome home ! Welcome home ! "

" Where are the children ? " said André Olsheffsky, brokenly. " Perhaps they're dead, too ? "

"Oh, the children are all well, *Barin!* They are at Volodia Ivanovitch's."

"Drive me there, then," said Mr. Olsheffsky; and the sledge dashed off with a peal of its bells, and drew up with a flourish in front of Volodia's doorway.

"Do look out, Elena!" cried Boris, who was carving a wooden man with an immense pocket-knife. "Here's a sledge stopped, and a funny tall gentleman getting out—not old, but all white!"

Elena went to the window, but the stranger had disappeared into the shop.

They could hear voices talking, now loud, now soft, then a cry of astonishment from Maria. The door burst open, and Volodia, his grey hair flying, the tears rolling down his cheeks, dragged in the white-haired gentleman by the hand.

"Oh, children! children! this is a happy day. The *Barin's* come home. This is your father!"

CHAPTER VIII.

The next morning Elena and Boris awoke with a delightful feeling of expectation.

It seemed impossible to realize that their father had really come back to them, and that he was dearer and kinder than anything they had imagined!

"If only mamma were here," sighed Elena, "*how* happy we should be!"

"Perhaps she knows," said Boris soberly. "She always told us papa was a hero, and I'm sure he looks like one."

André Olsheffsky felt his wife's loss deeply. The children were his only comfort, and every moment he could spare from his business affairs he gave to them.

With Elena he discussed their position seriously.

It would be impossible, he said, to prove their claim to Madame Olsheffsky's estate unless the lost box could be recovered, but if that were ever found the papers inside would completely establish their right. "I have sent notices to all the peasants, describing the box, and offering a reward. Who knows, Elena ? it *may* be discovered ! "

Time passed on, and though Mr. Olsheffsky made many expeditions into the town of Mourum, and drove all round the country, making enquiries of the peasants, he could hear nothing of the wooden box.

"It's one of the secrets of the lake," said Volodia. "That's my opinion ; it's lying snugly at the bottom there ; and it's no good looking for it anywhere else."

But Mr. Olsheffsky continued his enquiries.

One day, just as Daria and Var-Vara were about to start for a morning walk—Elena and Boris having gone for a drive with their father—an old man in a rough sheep-skin coat and plaited bark shoes came up to the house door, and taking off his high felt hat respectfully, asked if he could speak to the *Barin.**

* Master.

" The master has gone out," said Var-Vara, " but I dare-say you can see him in the afternoon. Have you anything particular to ask him ? "

" Nothing to ask, but something to show," and the old man blinked his eyes cunningly.

" Not the wooden box ! " screamed Daria. " Oh, let's go at once ! Come, Var-Vara ! *What* a surprise for papa when he gets back ! *Is* it the wooden box ? You might tell me," cried Daria, fixing her blue eyes on the old *mujik's* face pleadingly.

" It may be, and it mayn't be," replied the old man. " You may come along with me if you like, Daria Andreïevna. I'll show you the way to where I live—near the forest, you know. Of course, I've heard all about the reward," he continued, "and as I was clearing a bit of my yard this morning, what should I find but a heap of something hard—pebbles, and drift, and sticks, and such like. When I came to sorting it out—for I thought, ' Why waste good wood, when you can burn it ? the good God doesn't like waste '—I struck against the corner of something hard, and there was a ——. Well, what do you think, Daria Andreïevna ? "

" A box ! A box ! " cried Daria, seizing one of the old man's hands, and dancing round him in an ecstasy of delight.

" Not at all, Daria Andreïevna ! The legs of an old chair."

Daria's face fell. " I don't see why you come to tell papa you've found an old chair ! " she said crossly.

" Stop a bit, *Matoushka*. There's more to come. Where was I ? "

"The chair! You'd just found it," said Daria, pulling at his hand impatiently.

"So I had. A chair! Well, it had no back, and as I pulled it out it felt heavy, very heavy. It wasn't much to look at—a poor chair I should call it—and I thought, 'This isn't much of a find;' but there inside it was something sticking as tight as wax!"

"The box!" cried Daria, "I felt sure of it!" and seizing Var-Vara by one hand, and the *mujik* by the other, she dragged them down the street, the old peasant remonstrating and grumbling.

"Not so fast, Daria Andreïevna!" said Var-Vara, gasping for breath at the sudden rush. "Let Ivan go first; he knows the way!"

Daria could scarcely control her impatience during the walk.

"Make haste, Var-Vara! we shall never get there," she kept crying; and old Var-Vara, who was stout, and had on a heavy fur pelisse, arrived at the hut in a state of breathless exhaustion.

"Aïe! Aïe! what a child it is! Show her the box now, Ivan, or we shall have no peace."

Ivan went to the corner of his hut, where a large object stood on the top of the whitewashed stove under a red and yellow pocket-handkerchief. He carefully uncovered it, and stepping back a few paces said proudly,

"What do you think of *that*, now?"

It was the box, safe and unhurt, Madame Olsheffsky's name still on it in scratched white letters.

Daria was wild with joy, and almost alarmed Ivan with her excitement. She danced about the room, threw her arms round his neck, and finally persuaded him to carry the box to Volodia's house, so that it might be there as a delightful surprise to her father on his return.

CHAPTER IX.

The children, Volodia and his wife, Var-Vara, and Adam ; all stood round eagerly as André Olsheffsky superintended the forcing open of the precious box.

"It's my belief the papers will be a pulp," whispered Volodia. "We must be ready to stand by the *Barin* when he finds out the disappointment."

But the papers were not hurt. The box contained another tin-lined case, in which the parchments had lain securely, and though damaged in appearance, they were as legible as the day on which they were first written.

"Oh, papa, I *am* so glad ! " shouted Boris and Daria ; and Elena silently took her father's hand.

"I always thought the *Barin* would have his own again," cried Volodia triumphantly, forgetting that only a moment before he had been full of dismal prophecies.

Adam and Var-Vara wept for joy, and Ivan stood by smiling complacently. He felt that all this happiness had been brought about entirely by his own exertions, and he already had visions of the manner in which he would employ the handsome reward.

" No more troubling about my old age," he thought. " I shall have as comfortable a life as the best of them."

That evening Mr. Olsheffsky started for Moscow, carrying the parchments with him.

The two months of his absence seemed very long to the children, though they heard from him constantly ; and there were great rejoicings when he returned with the news that their affairs had at last been satisfactorily settled. Mikhail Paulovitch had withdrawn his claim, and the great house was their own again.

All the peasants of the neighbourhood came in a body to congratulate them. Those who could not get into Volodia's little sitting-room remained standing outside, and looked in respectfully through the window ; while the spokesman read a long speech he had prepared for the occasion.

Mr. Olsheffsky made an appropriate reply, and then, turning to Volodia and the old servants, he thanked them in a few simple words for their goodness to the children.

" You might have knocked me flat down with a birch twig," said Uncle Volodia afterwards, when talking it over with Adam. " The idea of thanking us for what was nothing at all but a real pleasure ! He's a good man, the *Barin !* "

The springtime found the children and their father settled once more in their old home, with Adam, Var-Vara, and

Alexis; and life flowing on very much as it had always done, except for the absence of the gentle, motherly, Anna Olsheffsky.

Uncle Volodia continued to look after his shop with zeal; and the two rooms with the gilt furniture, which Mr. Olsheffsky had insisted on his not removing, became objects of the greatest pride and joy to him.

He never allowed anyone but himself to dust them, and in spare moments he polished the looking-glass with a piece of leather, kept carefully for the purpose in a cigar box.

"It's a great pleasure to me," he remarked one day to a neighbour, "to think that when I leave this house to Boris Andreïevitch—as I intend to do, after old Maria—it will have two rooms that are fit for *any*one of the family to sleep in. He'll never have to be ashamed of *them!*"

On his seventieth birthday, Elena—now grown a tall slim young lady, with grave brown eyes—persuaded him that it was really time to take a little rest, and enjoy himself.

He thereupon sold his stock, and devoted himself to gardening in the yard at the back of his house; where he would sit on summer evenings smoking his pipe, in the midst of giant dahlias and sunflowers.

Here Daria often came with Boris and Tulipan; and sitting by Uncle Volodia's side, listened to the well-known stories she had heard since her babyhood—always ending up with the same words in a tone of great solemnity— "And *this*, children, is a true story, every word of it!"

The Angel and the Lilies.

A NORWEGIAN STORY.

IT was a room at the top of a rough woo.len house in Norway. Though it was only a garret, it was all very white and clean : and little Erik Svenson lay in the small bed facing the barred window, through which the moonbeams streamed till they seemed to turn the walls into polished silver.

As Erik tossed about, he heard his mother working in the room below.

The *thump, thump,* of her iron, as she wearily finished the last of the clothes, that must be sent home to the rich family at the farmhouse, early next morning.

" Poor mother! how hard she works," thought Erik, " and *I* can't do more than mind Farmer Torvald's boat on the fiord. If I could only be employed in the town, I might be able to help her ! "

Thump, thump, went the iron. The clock chimed twelve, and still the poor washerwoman smoothed and folded, though her heavy eyes almost refused to keep open, and the room began to feel the chill of the frosty air outside.

G

" Erik sha'n't want for anything while I have two arms to work for him," she said to herself; and went on until the iron fell from her tired hand, and she sank back in her chair in a deep sleep.

Erik, too, had closed his eyes, and was dreaming happily, when he was awakened by the brush of something light and soft, across his pillow.

Starting up, he saw that the moon was still brilliant, and in its clearest rays stood a faint white figure, with shadowy wings outstretched behind it.

A vapoury garment enveloped it, and the face seemed young and beautiful.

" Oh, how wonderful! How wonderful you are!" cried Erik. " Why have I never seen you before ? "

" I am Vanda, the Spirit of the Moon," said the Angel gently. " Only to those who are in need of help can I become visible. Your mother knows me well. Winter and summer, I have soothed her to sleep ; and to-night, as you looked from the window, your thoughts joined mine, and I was able to come to you. What will you ask of me ? "

" Oh, Vanda, dear Vanda ! Show me how to help my mother ; I ask nothing else ! " cried Erik.

He jumped from his bed, and threw himself at the feet of the shadowy Angel.

" Do you see that window ? " said the Moon-Spirit, pointing to the small panes that were now covered with a delicate

tracery of glittering frost-work. "Of what do those patterns remind you ? "

"Of flowers ! " cried Erik. "I have often thought so. Sometimes I can see grasses, and boughs, and roses, but *always* lilies, because they are so white and spotless."

The Angel smiled softly.

"To-night I shall shine upon them, and make them live," she said. "Take what you will find upon the window sill at sunrise, and sell them in the town. Bring the money back to your mother at night-time."

With the last words the Moon-Spirit melted into the white light, leaving Erik with a feeling of the happiest expectation.

Long before daybreak he was awake, and his first thought was of the wonderful ice-flowers. Would the Angel have kept her promise ? What would he see awaiting him ?

As the rays of the sun shot over the fiord, he sprang out of bed and ran to the window. There lay a bunch of beautiful white lilies, nestling in a mass of delicate moss-like green.

"They *are* the frost-flowers ! " cried Erik, and wild with joy he rushed into his mother's room, and held the bunch up for her to look at.

"Look, look, mother! See what we have had given us. We shall soon have enough money to rent the little farm you have always been longing for ! "

*   *   *

Erik's visit to the town was very successful. He sold his flowers directly, although he had some difficulty in answering all the questions of the townspeople, who wanted to know where he had grown such delicate things in the middle of a severe winter. To everyone he replied that it was a secret; and they were obliged to be contented.

He returned home in good time for his work upon the fiord, and if it had not been for the store of silver pieces he poured into his mother's work-box, he would almost have imagined that he had only been dreaming.

That night, as he laid his curly head upon the pillow, his mind was full of thoughts about the Moon-Angel. He wondered if she would appear again, and whether she would once more leave him her gift of the white frost-flowers.

The moon shone with silvery clearness into the garret; and as the boy strained his eyes towards the window, the bright form slowly floated through the bars and stretched a pale hand towards him.

" You have done well, to-day, Erik. Look tomorrow, and tomorrow, and tomorrow, until my light has waned and faded ; and every day you will find the lilies waiting for you."

Again Erik felt the soft brush of Vanda's wings, and she disappeared in the path of the moonbeams.

The next morning the flowers lay fresh and fair upon the window-sill, and for days the frost-lilies were always blooming.

But each time the bunch grew smaller and smaller, until

at last, when the moon was nothing more than a thread of brightness, Erik found one single blossom lying half drooping on the window-frame.

"Vanda's gifts have ended," thought Erik, "but she has been a good true friend to us! We have gained enough money for my mother to put away her iron, and take the little farmhouse by the fiord. How happy we shall be together."

The winter was nearly over, and Erik and his mother had settled down to their happy life in the farmhouse.

Frost-flowers, with delicate fantastic groupings, still bloomed upon the window-panes; but the Moon-Angel was not there to give them her fairy-like gifts of life and beauty.

She had gone to console other struggling workers.

The Alpen=Echo.

LONG, long years ago, a young girl wandering with her herd of goats upon the Mettenalp, lost her way amidst a mountain storm, and fell into a chasm of the rock, where she lay white and lifeless.

The terrified goats reached the valley beneath, but the young girl was never again heard of.

The spirits of the great mountain had claimed her for an Alpen-Echo, and every day, for hundreds of years after, she floated amongst the snow-covered peaks and crags of the Mettenalp, answering every horn that sounded from the hunters or cow-herds, with a soft, sweet note, so sad and distant it was like a soul in pain, and tears came to your eyes—you knew not why—as you listened to its exquisite music.

"Come, follow me! Follow me to my secret haunts," wailed the Echo. "Give me my soul! Give me my soul!"—but no one through all the centuries had ever climbed to the Echo's hiding-place.

"If *only* I could make them understand!" sobbed the Echo,

"my long bondage would cease. The first foot that treads my prison, frees me, and gives me rest."

✻   ✻   ✻   ✻   ✻   ✻

However, all the world was too busy to listen to the poor Echo, and she called and cried in vain through the misty ages!

✻   ✻   ✻   ✻

A boy, with a long Alpen-horn in his hand, stood by a châlet far away in the wilds of Switzerland. Every now and then he blew a few wailing notes upon the horn—notes that echoed across the valley, up to the snow-covered heights beyond—and he smiled as the answer floated clearly back again.

"The echoes are talking together, to-day," he said to himself. "They love the bright air and the sunshine;" and again he blew a long, changing note, that died away softly into the far distance.

"*Tra-la-la-a-a*" came faintly from the opposite mountain— but to the boy's astonishment the echo did not now cease, and fade away, as it always had done before. It shifted from point to point; its elfin tones ringing sweet and sad like the bugle of a Fairy Huntsman.

All that day the Echo sounded in the boy's ears, all night it whispered amongst the mountain tops; and as soon as it became daylight he sprang up, determined that he would climb the side of the opposite valley, and find out the reason of the strange music.

A pale-green light tinged the sky, the mountains looked dark and forbidding, and from the peaks above came the soft sighing of the distant Echo.

"It is like a soul in pain," thought the boy. "I *must* find out what it means!" and he began to climb higher and higher, until the valley lay far beneath him, and his home looked a little brown speck amidst a sea of fields and pine trees.

Before him still sounded the Elfin voice, now dying into a whisper, now ringing clear and distinct, as though close beside him—but always with the same beseeching sadness: "Follow me! Follow me to my secret haunts! Give me my soul! Give me my soul!" And the boy climbed on until he reached the rocky crag which formed the summit of the mountain.

"At last!" he cried, as he stretched out his arms to clasp the Echo's fairy-like form that floated mistily before him . . . but the Echo had faded from his sight as he approached her; and her last words were borne faintly towards him as she vanished into the golden glory of the sunshine—

"At last! At last! I am at rest at last!"

     ❋   ❋   ❋

The boy had learnt the secret of the Alpen-Echo. He had freed her soul from its long bondage, and a few days afterwards they found him lying with a smile upon his face on the topmost peak of the Mettenalp.

The Scroll in the Market Place.

IN the pale light of the moon the sleeping town lay hushed and noiseless. At its foot the river rolled, spanned by the curves of the old grey stone bridge, and behind rose the giant hills, clothed with tracts of pine and birch trees. A high wall surrounded the town, with towers at intervals, from which gleamed the light of the watchmen's lanterns.

All was silent on the earth and in the air, when through the deep blue of the star-sprinkled sky a little Child-Angel winged his way from Heaven, and hovering over the steep red roofs beneath him, folded his wings and dropped softly into the deserted Market Place. In his hand he held a Scroll with strange writing upon it, and crossing the Square over the rough cobble-stones, he fixed the paper to the Fountain, and spreading his white wings, flew up again to the home from which he came.

Next day the country people flocking into the Market Place saw to their astonishment a track of beautiful white flowers springing up from amongst the cobble-stones, and stretching from one corner of the Square to the Fountain.

They were star-like flowers, with bright-green leaves, and they grew in patches—"like a child's footsteps," the women said.

A little crowd soon gathered round the paper fastened to the ancient Fountain. On the top of the Scroll was written, very clearly—"All those who can read the words beneath shall be rewarded generously," but the lines that followed were in a strange language, and in such crabbed characters that they defied every effort to decipher them.

All day the crowd ebbed and flowed round the Fountain, while the learned men of the town came with their dictionaries under their arms and spectacles on nose, and sat on stools, attempting to make out the crooked letters of the inscription.

In the end each one decided upon a different language, and the argument became so warm between them that they had to be separated by a party of watchmen, and conducted back again to their own houses.

Professors from the University on the other side of the mountains journeyed over the rough roads, and brought their learning to the old stone Fountain in the Market Place—but they, too, went away discomfited.

No one could read the strange writing, and no one could pull down the paper, for it appeared to be fixed to the stone by some means that made it impossible to tear it away.

Time went on, and the snow covered up the Market Square, threw a white mantle over the steep roofs, and buried the old gardens in its soft deepness.

In one of the houses near the spot where the little Angel had first touched the earth lived a poor, lonely woman. She worked all day at some fine kind of needlework, but when, in the evenings, the sun had set and the twilight began to fall, she would steal out for a few minutes to breathe the fresh air. Often, though she was so wearied with her incessant stitching, she would carry in her hand a flower from the plants that grew in her latticed window to a neighbour's sick child. It was a weary climb up a steep flight of stairs to the attic where the sick child lay, but it was reward enough to the woman to see the bright smile that lighted up the little drawn face as she laid the flower on the counterpane.

All the summer the poor sempstress had been too busy during the daylight, to afford time even to cross the Square to study the strange paper on the Fountain. "If learned men cannot read it, a poor ignorant woman like me could certainly never do so," she said to the child, and the little girl looked up at her with tender love in her eyes.

"You are so good, you could do *anything*," she whispered, and clasped the worn hand on which the needle-pricks had left the marks of many long years of patient sewing. "I should like to see the paper so much," continued the child, after a thoughtful pause. "I wish I could walk there, but it is so long since I walked, and the snow is so deep now," and she sighed.

"Some day, if the good God pleases, I will carry you there," said the workwoman—and the child as she lay

patiently on her little bed, dreamt and dreamt of the
mysterious paper that no one could read, until the longing
to see it became uncontrollable, and her friend the sempstress
promised that she would spare an hour the next day from
her work, and if the sun shone she would carry the invalid
across the Market Place to the old stone Fountain.

The next morning the child's face was bright with antici-
pation, as the woman wrapped her in a warm shawl and
carried her fragile weight down the staircase. The cobble-
stones hurt the poor sempstress's feet, and she staggered
under the light burden, but she persevered, for the child's
murmurs of delight rang in her ears—

" How sweetly the sun shines! How white the snow
looks! How beautiful, how *beautiful* it is to be alive! "

When they reached the Fountain the sun shone brightly
upon the Angel's Scroll.

The workwoman seated herself on one of the swept stone
steps, still holding the child in her arms, and they gazed
long and earnestly at the writing above them.

Gradually a smile of delight spread across both their
faces. " It is quite, *quite* easy! " they cried together.
" How is it people have been puzzling so long ? "—for as
they looked the crabbed letters unrolled before them,
straightened, and arranged themselves in order, and the
Angel's message was read by the poor workwoman and
the sick child.

" Love God, and live for others," said the Scroll, and a

soft light seemed to stream from it and shed a glow of
happiness right into the hearts of the two who read it.   The
air was warmer, the sun shone more brightly, and just by
the foot of the Fountain, pushing through the snow, sprang
one blue head of palest forget-me-not.

As the letters on the Scroll became plainer and plainer,
the paper slowly rolled up an 1 shrunk away, until it had
disappeared altogether.

The sempstress carried back the child up the steep staircase, laid her tenderly on her bed, and hurried away to her
own attic.

In her absence strange things had happened.   The room
was swept and tidy, the flowers were watered, and the piece
of work she had left half done was lying finished on the broad
window seat.   The poor woman looked round her in astonishment.   She went downstairs to enquire if any neighbours
had prepared this surprise for her, but they only stared at
her. and told her " she must have left her wits in the Market
Place," and that " that was what came of leaving your own
duties to look after other people's."

The sempstress did not listen to their taunts, for a song
of joy was welling up in her heart—a song so sweet and
true, it might have been the echo of that sung by the angels.
Never had life seemed so beautiful to her.   The ill looks of
the neighbours appeared to her to be smiles of kindness and
love ; their hard speeches sounded soft and altered ; the
steep stairs to her room were not so steep, her attic not so

bare and desolate. Life was no longer lonely, for the song in her heart brought her all the happiness she had ever hoped for.

The sick child, too, found the same wonderful change in all that surrounded her. The aunt with whom she lived, who had always been so careless and unloving, now seemed to the child to be kind and gentle. Her aching back was less painful, her thoughts as she lay on her bed were bright and happy. The Angel's message had brought sunshine to the lives of the only two who could read and understand it.

* * *

In time the sick child went to live with the sempstress, and their love for each other grew and strengthened, and overflowed in a thousand little acts of kindness to all who came near them. Their room was filled with brightness. The birds flew to perch on the window-sill and sing in the early mornings; flowers bloomed in the cracks of the old stonework; the sempstress sang as she worked, and whenever she left her sewing to carry the child out into the Market Place to breathe the fresh air she would find her work finished when she returned.

"It was a happy day that we read the message in the Market Place," she said to the sick child; "indeed we have been rewarded generously."

A Scrap of Etruscan Pottery.

DEEP down in a buried Etruscan tomb there lay a little three-cornered piece of pottery.

It had some letters on it and a beautiful man's head, and had belonged to a King some three thousand years ago.

Its only companions were a family of moles; for everything else had been taken out of the tomb so long ago that no one remembered anything about it.

"What a dull life mine is," groaned the piece of pottery. "No amusement, and no society! It's enough to make one smash oneself to atoms!"

"Dull, but safe," replied the Mole, who never took the least notice of the three-cornered Chip's insults. "And then, remember the dignity. You have the whole tomb to yourself."

"Except for you," said the Chip ungraciously.

"Well, we must live somewhere," said the Mole, quite unmoved, "and I'm sure we don't interfere. I always bring up my children to treat you with the greatest respect, in spite of your being cr-r—br-r—. I *should* say, not quite so large as you used to be."

"If only you had belonged to a King," sighed the Chip, "I might have had someone of my own class to talk to."

"I don't wish to belong to a King," said the Mole. "There's nothing I should dislike more. I am for a Liberal Government, and no farming."

"What vulgarity!" cried the Chip.

"It's a blessing it's dark, and he can't see the children laughing," thought the Mole-mother, "or I don't know what would happen."

"Everything that belonged to a King should be treated with Royal respect," continued the Chip.

"As to that, I really haven't time for it," replied the Mole; "what with putting the children to bed, and getting them up again, and all my work in the passages, I can't devote myself to Court life."

"If you like, you can represent the people," said the Chip. "I don't mind, only then I can't talk to you."

"You can read out Royal Decrees, and make laws," said the Mole; and to herself she added, "It won't disturb me. I shan't take any notice of them."

"Who's to be nobles?" said the Chip, crossly. "I'd rather not do the thing at all, if it can't be done properly!"

"Well, I can't be people and nobles too, that's quite certain," remarked the Mole-mother, as she tidied up her house. "Besides, the children are too young—they wouldn't understand."

"What's it like up above?" enquired the Chip languidly

after a short pause, for it was almost better to speak to the
Mole, than to nobody. " People still walk on two legs ? "
" Why, of course," answered the Mole, " there's never any
difference in people, that *I* can see. They're always exactly
alike, except in tempers."

The Chip was sitting upon a little stone-heap against one
of the pillars. He fondly imagined it was a Throne ; and
the Mole-mother, with the utmost good nature, had never
undeceived him.

As the last words were spoken, a lump of earth fell from
the roof, flattening out the stone-heap, and the Chip only
escaped destruction by rolling on one side, where he lay
shaking with fright and calling to the Mole-mother to help
him. But the Mole had retired with her family to a place
of safety. She knew what was happening. The tomb was
being opened by a party of antiquarians, and in a few more
minutes the blue sky shone into the darkness, and the three-
cornered piece of pottery was lying wrapped in paper in the
pocket of one of the explorers.

*   *   *   *   *

When the Chip recovered himself, he found he was
reclining on the velvet floor of a large glass case full of
Etruscan vases. Here was the society he had been pining
for all his life !

" What are Moles compared to this ? " he said to him-

H

self, and quivered with joy at the thought of the pleasures
before him.

" How did that broken thing come into our Division ? "
enquired a Red Dish with two handles.

" I can't imagine ! The Director put him in just now,"
replied a Black Jug. " It's not what we're accustomed to.
Everything in here is perfect."

The Chip lay for a moment, dumb with horror and
astonishment.

" I belonged to a King," he gasped at last. " You can
look at the name written on me."

" You may have names written all over you, for all I care,"
said the Dish. " You're a Chip, and no King can make you
anything else "—and she turned away haughtily.

" And to think that for all those years the Mole-mother
was never once rude to me ! " thought the Chip. " She was
a person of *real* refinement. Whatever shall I do if I have
to be shut up with these ill-bred people ? " he groaned
miserably.

" How the woodwork does creak ! " said the Director as
he came up to the glass case, with a young lady to whom he
was showing the treasures of the Museum.

" That's the most recent discovery," he continued smiling
and pointing to the three-cornered piece of pottery—" All
I found in my last digging."

" It has a beautiful head on it," said the young lady, " I
should be quite satisfied if I could ever find anything so pretty."

"Will you have it?" said the Director of the Museum, who after all was only a young man; looking at the young lady earnestly.

She took the despised Chip in her little hand.

"Thank you very much. It will be a great treasure," she said—and looking up at her face, the three-cornered piece of pottery knew that a happy life was in store for him.

* * * * * *

"In spite of the rudeness of my own people, I am in the Museum after all," remarked the Chip, as some months afterwards he hung on a bracket on the wall of the young lady's sitting room. "In what a superior position, too! *They* only belong to the Director, but *I* belong to the Director's wife!"

The Goats on the Glacier.

CHAPTER I.

THE Heif Goats lived close to the Heifen Glacier, one of the largest in Switzerland. In fact, their Châlet, or the cavern which they christened by that name, overhung the steepest precipice, and was inaccessible to anyone except its proprietors.

"It is such a comfort to be secluded in these disturbed times," the Goat-mother often remarked to her husband. "If I lived near a high road I should never know a *moment's* happiness. The children are so giddy, they would be gambolling about round the very wheels of the char-à-bancs, turning head over heels for halfpence, before I could cry Goats-i-tivy!"

The whole glacier valley swarmed with the kin of the Goat family. There were the bond-slaves who worked for the peasants, and the free Goats who possessed their own caves, cultivated their ground industriously, and lived greatly on the sandwich papers left by tourists in the summer-time.

"Such a treat, especially the light yellow sort with printing, that always has crumbs in it," said the Goat-mother. "It makes a delicious meal. We generally have it on fête days."

The family of the Heif Goats consisted of the Heif-father, his wife, and their four children, Heinrich, Lizbet, Pyto, and Lénora.

The young Goats had been brought up with some severity by their parents, who had old-fashioned notions with regard to discipline; and three things had been especially enjoined upon them from their infancy. Always to speak the truth, never to mess their clean pinafores, and last, but not least, *never* to play with the Chamois!

" They are too wild and frivolous," the Goat-mother used to say, with a nod of her frilled cap. " Such very long springs are in exceedingly bad taste. The Chamois have *no* repose of manner."

Under this system the children grew up very well-behaved. The daughters worked in the house, the sons helped their father; and in the evening they all descended to the Glacier to collect any remnants of food left by the endless stream of visitors, who all through the summer toiled up to the Eismeer, and down again to the Inn on the other side of the valley.

These travellers were a perpetual source of interest and amusement to the Goat family.

They could never quite make out what they were doing, but the Heif-mother finally decided that their journeys must be some religious or national observance.

" People would never struggle about on the ice like that—

tied to each other with ropes, too!—unless it was a painful
duty," she said. " I consider it very praiseworthy."

Sometimes the young Goats in their invisible eyrie, would
go off into shouts of merriment as a group of excursionists
crawled slowly into sight; the ladies in their short skirts
and large flapping hats, alpenstock in hand, clinging
desperately to the guides as they ascended every slippery
ice-peak.

But on these occasions the Goat-mother always reproved
them.

" Remember," she would say severely, " that because
people are ridiculous you shouldn't be unmannerly. They
can't help their appearance, poor things! They may think
themselves quite as good as we are."

" Well, at all events, we don't look like *that*," said Lizbet. " I am sure you would never allow it."

The principal news from the outer world was brought to
the Heif family by a Stein-bok pedlar, who wandered about
the country with his wares, and was so popular that he was
a friend of all classes, and supplied even the Chamois with
their groceries and tobacco.

He generally arrived at the Châlet on the first of every
month, and spread out his wares on the grass plot in front
of the cave, while the Goat-mother and her children walked
up and down, and bargained good-humouredly for anything
they had taken a fancy to.

CHAPTER II.

It was a bright sunny day, and the Goat-mother sat with her daughters at the door of the cavern. The Goat-father had gone off by himself to get some provisions at a village on the opposite side of the Glacier, and Heinrich and Pyto were digging in the fields at the back of the Châlet; when the Stein-bok, in his well-known brown cloth coat, appeared panting up the narrow pathway.

Throwing himself down on a stone bench, he tossed his Tyrolese hat on to the ground, and fanned himself with his handkerchief.

"Good morning, Herr Stein-bok. You seem exhausted," said the Goat-mother.

"I am, ma'am, and well I may be. Five miles with twenty pounds on my back is no joke, I can assure you."

"Shall I bring you a glass of lager-beer?" enquired the Heif-mother.

"It would be acceptable, ma'am, and then I will tell you my news. You've heard nothing of the Goat-father, have you?"

"Nothing," said the Goat-mother. "I am beginning to feel very nervous. I never knew him to stay away two days before."

The Stein-bok looked round darkly.

"I have something to tell you," he whispered. "Prepare for bad news. The Goat-father has been captured."

The Heif-mother gave a wild shriek, and fell back upon Lizbet, who was peeling potatoes in the doorway.

"When—where—how—who—what?" she cried frantically.
"Tell me at once, or I shall faint away."

"Be calm, ma'am," said the Stein-bok soothingly. "I
heard it from the Chamois, who have a habit of bounding
about everywhere, as you know. Your dear husband reached
the middle of the Glacier in safety, when—being hampered
by a satchel and a green cotton umbrella—he fell in attempting to jump an ice-pinnacle, and sprained his foot so severely
that he was unable to move. Though he bleated loudly for
help, no one came except some huntsmen who were in search
of Chamois. They picked him up, and dragged him to the
Inn on the other side of the valley, where he was locked up
securely in a shed, and there he is at the present moment."

"My brave Heif in prison! He will never, never survive
it!" cried the Goat-mother, shedding tears in profusion.

"Oh yes he will, ma'am," replied the Stein-bok, "they're
not going to kill him, their idea is to take him down to the
village."

"_That_ they shall never do!" cried the Heif-mother, starting
up, "not if I go myself to rescue him! Go, Lizbet, and call
your brothers. We must consult together immediately."

Lizbet darted off, and the Stein-bok continued.

"I have still something else I must let you know, ma'am.
As our great poet observes—

'Whenever green food fades away,
      Some dire misfortune comes the self-same day.'

In plain words, troubles never come singly. I discovered
while having a friendly game of dominoes with
the Head Chamois, that they intend to seize
upon your house next Tuesday, in the
absence of the Heif-father."
"And to-day is Friday!"
shrieked the Goat-
mother. "Oh!
this is hard
indeed!"

"Compose yourself, ma'am, and listen to my advice," said the Pedlar. "You lock up your house, or leave me in charge with Lizbet and Lénora, and you and the two other children start off at once to ask the help of the Goat-king. He is a mild, humane creature, and will very likely order out a detachment of the ' Free-will ' goats to help to defend your household."

"That is the only thing to do," said the Goat-mother mournfully. "I certainly know the way, for of course I have always been to the yearly Goat Assembly, but I always started three days before the meeting, and went down the back of the mountain, over the slopes. I don't know how I'm to manage the short cut."

"Oh, easy enough, ma'am," replied the Stein-bok ; "you'll get on very well. Don't go in goloshes, though, for they will be sure to catch on the nails. I wouldn't wear my waterproof mantle either—too large for a walking tour. Put on a shawl, and tie it round you."

By this time Heinrich and Pyto had hastily dressed themselves in out-door costume, and the Goat-mother was rushing about her house, collecting an extraordinary number of things, which the Stein-bok had some difficulty in persuading her not to take with her.

"*Not* sugar nippers, ma'am, I *beg* ; or your large workbox, or the mincing machine ! Quite useless on a long journey ; and your best cap you won't want, I assure you."

"I thought I might perhaps wait a moment in the ante-

room and put it on before entering the presence of Royalty,"
bleated the Goat-mother.. " But no doubt you know best."

The luggage was at last reduced to a small leather handbag ; and the Goat-mother, after solemnly bestowing her
blessing on Lizbet and Lénora, and the door-key on the
Stein-bok, set off down the garden path with her children,
upon their adventures.

CHAPTER III.

Meanwhile, the Goat-father was languishing in a dark
shed attached to the Inn on the other side of the Glacier.
His bleats had failed to attract any attention. In fact the
only person who had heard him at all, had been an old Goat-
slave, who while browsing on the hillside with a bell round
his neck, had been attracted by the cries, and creeping up to
the shed, peeped through a crack to see what could be the
matter.

" Is there anyone near ? " enquired the Goat-father in a
whisper.

" No. There's a party in the Inn, but they are too busy
eating to take any notice of us. I am just loitering here, in
case there should be any pieces of sandwich paper flying
about."

"Is there any chance of my making my escape ? " enquired
the Heif-father. " Are they very watchful people ? "

"Excessively so," replied the old Slave. "I've never been able to get away for the last ten years."

The Goat-father groaned. "Then it wouldn't be possible for you to take a message to my family?"

"Quite impossible, my dear friend, I assure you. Can't you find any crack in the shed where you could break through?"

"There's *nothing*," cried the Goat-father. "I've searched round and round, and the door is as strong and tight as a prison."

"Well, I'll go off and see if I can find a messenger," said the old Slave good-naturedly. "Perhaps the old fox would manage it."

"A fox! Oh, I don't think *that* would do," said the Heif-father. "It mightn't be safe for my family."

"Oh, *he's* all right," said the Slave. "He's been in captivity so long, it's taken all the spirit out of him. He might live in a farmyard. He's a good-natured creature, too, and I daresay he'll go to oblige me."

The Goat-father pulled a band and buckle off his necktie, and poked it under the door.

"Not to eat!" he whispered warningly, "but for the fox to take with him, that my wife may know the message comes from me; and be quick about it, my good friend, for I really am positively starving!"

"All right," said the old Goat, "I'll send the fox off, and come back in a few minutes to bring you some stale cabbage leaves."

" A friend in need, is a friend indeed!" murmured the Goat-father; and went to sleep that night with more hope than he had felt since the moment of his capture.

CHAPTER IV.

"Come along, mother," cried Heinrich, grasping the Heif-mother's hand as they left the garden before their Châlet, and commenced the dangerous descent of the mountain.

Far below them they could see the great stretch of the dazzlingly white Glacier, with its rents and fissures shining greenly in the sunshine. On either side rose bare crags topped with grass, and above all, the snowy summits of the mountains.

The first part of the journey led along a narrow pathway, which the Goat-mother managed very successfully, but when they came to the precipice on which rough iron spikes had been driven at long intervals to assist the climber, her heart failed her, and in spite of her desire to hurry, she entangled her shawl and dress so constantly on the nails, that her children began to fear she would never reach the level of the Glacier.

At last, however, the little party succeeded in making their way across the Eismeer, and arrived without further mishap at the river leading to the Goat-King's Palace.

This river flowed on the centre of the Glacier, between

steep banks of transparent ice, every now and again disappearing into some vast cavern, where it swept with a hollow echoing under the ice-field.

"Follow me, mother," said Heinrich. "I see the entrance to the Palace just in front of us."

The Goat-mother gathered up her skirts, and assisted by Pyto, began to scramble down the bank to the side of the streamlet.

"Where is the boat kept?" she enquired.

"In a snowdrift close to the entrance," replied Heinrich. "Don't jump about near the crevasses, Pyto, and I'll go and fetch it."

The boat was soon dragged from its hiding place, and Heinrich paddled it to the spot where the Goat-mother was resting on a snow-bank.

She embarked with some nervousness, clutching desperately at her handbag. They pushed off, and were immediately carried by the current through the little round opening of the cave into the pale green glistening depths of the mysterious world beyond.

CHAPTER V.

There was no need for the Heif family to row. They were swept along past the ice walls, and in a few minutes reached the Goat-King's landing-place. A small inlet with a flat shore, on which were arranged two camp stools and a piece of red carpet.

"Here we are at last, dear children," said the Goat-mother. "What a relief it is, to be sure! Is my bonnet straight, Pyto? and do pull your blouse down. Your hair is all standing on end, Heinrich! How I wish the Stein-bok had allowed me to bring a pocket-comb!"

The Court Porter, seated in a bee-hive chair, came forward as soon as he saw them, to ask their business.

"The Goat-King is at home to-day till five o'clock," he said. "If you will step this way, I will introduce you immediately."

The Goat-mother trembling in every limb—for she had never had a private interview with Royalty before—clutched a child in each hand and followed the Porter.

They passed down two passages, and finally reached a large ice-grotto, with a row of windows opening on to a wide crevasse.

The room was filled with a flickering green light that yet rendered everything distinctly visible.

On a carved maple chair on the top of a dias sat the Goat-King—a snow-white Goat with mauve eyes and beard: completely surrounded with cuckoo clocks, and festoons of yellow wood table-napkin rings, and paper-cutters. The walls seemed to be covered with them, and the pendulums of the clocks were swinging in every direction.

"The King thinks it right to patronize native art," said

the Goat-Queen, who with three of the Princesses had come
forward graciously to welcome the visitors.

" I find the striking rather trying at times, especially as
they don't all do it at once, and sometimes one cuckoo
hasn't finished *ten* before the others are at *twelve* again."

" I wish all the works would go wrong ! " muttered one
of the Princesses crossly. " An ice-cavern full of cuckoo
clocks is a poor fate for one of the Royal Family ! "

" We *must* encourage industries," said the Queen. " It
is a duty of our position. I should rather the industries
were noiseless, but we can't choose."

" Bead necklaces and Venetian glass would have been
more suitable," said the Princess, who had been very well
educated, " or even brass-work and embroidered table-cloths.
We might have draped the cavern with *them*."

At this moment there was a violent whirring amongst the
clocks ; doors flew open in all directions, and cuckoos of
every size and description darted out, shook themselves
violently, and the air was filled with such a deafening noise
that the Goat-mother threw her apron over her head, and
the Goat-children buried their ears in her skirts, and clung
round her in terror.

" Merely four o'clock ; nothing to make such a fuss
about," said the Goat-King. " And now, when we can
hear ourselves speak, you shall tell me what you have
come for."

As the voice of the last cuckoo died away in a series of

jerks, the Goat-mother advanced, and threw herself on her knees before the Royal Family, first spreading out her homespun apron to keep the cold off.

The King listened to her tale with interest, and his mauve eyes sparkled.

"If this is true," he cried fiercely, "the Chamois shall be crushed! My official pen, Princess; and a large sheet of note paper!"

"Rest yourself, petitioner, you must be tired," said the Queen, and pointed to a row of carved and inlaid Tyrolese chairs that stood against the wall.

The Goat-mother and her children seated themselves gratefully, and as they did so, a burst of music floated upon the air, several tunes struggling together for the mastery.

"Yes; it's very unpleasant, isn't it?" said the Goat-Queen, seeing the expression of surprise and uneasiness that showed itself on the visitors' faces. "We're obliged to have all the chairs made like that, to encourage the trade in musical boxes. I get very tired of it, I assure you, and I often stand up all day, just for the sake of peace and quietness. I really *dread* sitting down!"

Meanwhile, the Goat-King was busily writing, covering his white paws with ink in the process; and the Queen, in a very loud voice to make herself heard, was conversing with the Goat-mother about her household affairs.

"Supplies are most difficult to procure in this secluded spot," she said mournfully. "Would you believe me, that

I

last week we dined *every* day off boiled Geneva newspapers
and cabbage? So monotonous, and the King gets quite
angry ! "

" I wish we could live on boiled cuckoos!" cried the eldest
Princess, who with her sisters was seated on a bench by the
window, spinning; the pale green light of the Glacier shining
upon their white dresses, and the little brown spinning-wheels
that whirred so rapidly before them.

" Petitioner, the order is ready," said the King at this
moment, waving a large envelope. " Go straight home,
and send this paper round to all the Goats of the neighbourhood. It is an order to the ' Free-will ' Goats, to arm,
and assemble at your house for the defence of your family,
and the rescue of the Heif-father."

The Goat-mother curtsied to the ground, kissed the Queen's
hand, and retired with Heinrich and Pyto through the
passages to the landing place.

At the last moment one of the Princesses came running
after the Goat-mother, to press a cuckoo clock upon her, as
a parting present from the Queen.

The clock was large, and they had some difficulty in getting
it into the boat, but the Goat-mother did not dare to refuse it.

With the Porter's help they got off at last, and started
upon the return voyage, Heinrich and Pyto rowing their
hardest; for the current swept through the ice-caves with
such force that the Goat-mother had some difficulty in
steering.

As they came out into the daylight, they saw that the sun was almost setting, and a faint pink light tinged the snow-fields, and the tops of the distant mountains.

"We must hurry, or we shan't be back by nightfall!" said the Goat-mother nervously; and they landed on an ice-block, covered up the boat again in its hiding place, and set off towards home, across the Glacier.

CHAPTER VI.

The weary travellers almost sank with fatigue as they stumbled over the rough ice.

In addition to the handbag, they now had the cuckoo clock, and though Heinrich had insisted on carrying it strapped on his back like a knapsack, his mother could see that he became more and more exhausted, and at last she determined on taking it from him and carrying it herself.

The difficulty was heightened by the fact that the clock continued to tick, and the cuckoo to bound out of the door at unexpected moments, startling the Goat-mother so, that she almost dropped it.

"It's the shaking that puts its works out," said Heinrich. "Hold on tight, mother, and we shall get it home safely at last!"

"I wish it was at the bottom of the Glacier!" groaned the

Goat-mother, staggering along; her bonnet nearly falling off, her shawl trailing on the snow behind her.

"Be careful, Pyto! Careless Goat!" she cried. "Test the snow-bridges carefully with your alpenstock before you venture on them!"

But Pyto, who was young and giddy, went gamboling on; until suddenly, without even time for a bleat of terror, he fell crashing through the rotten ice, and disappeared from view into one of the largest crevasses.

"Goats-i-tivy!" cried the Goat-mother. "He's gone! Oh, my darling child, where are you?"

The cuckoo clock was thrown aside, and she ran to the edge of the crack and peered down frantically.

"All right, mother," said a voice, sounding very faint and hollow, "I've stuck in a hole. Let me down something, and perhaps I can scramble out again."

"What have we got to let down?" said the Goat-mother. "Not a ball of string amongst us! Oh, if ever we go on a journey again, I'll never, *never* listen to the Stein-bok."

"Well, mother, we must make the best of what we have," cried Heinrich. "Take your shawl off and tear it into strips. We *may* be able to make a rope long enough to reach him—anyhow we'll try!"

The Goat-mother consented eagerly, though her shawl was one she was particularly fond of. She snatched it off, and taking out her scissors, she soon cut it into pieces, which Heinrich knotted one to the other, and lowered into the crevasse.

"Can you reach it ?" he cried, putting his head as far over the edge as possible, and peering into the green depths.

The Goat-mother leant over, too; but in stooping her head her bonnet became loosened, and slid with a loud *swish* down the ice, darting from side to side until it disappeared from sight in the darkness.

"Oh, what misfortunes ! My child, my shawl, and my bonnet, *all* gone together !" she cried, wringing her hands. "Take hold of the rope, my Pyto, and let us at all events rescue *you !*"

" All right, mother," cried the distant voice. "Don't drag me up till I call out ' *Pull.*' "

In a few minutes the Goat-mother and Heinrich, listening intently, heard the welcome shout, and pulling both together they landed Pyto—very much bruised and shaken, but not otherwise hurt—upon the Glacier beside them.

"Oh, what a warning !" cried the Goat-mother, and after embracing Pyto warmly, she turned to look for the cuckoo clock. But it had tobogganned down a steep bank into an ice stream close by, and was floating away in the distance, *cuckooing* at intervals as it danced up and down upon the water.

Two travellers who had just reached the opposite bank, paused in astonishment to listen.

" You see," said one, " this proves what I have always told you. Nothing is impossible to Nature. You may even hear cuckoos on a Glacier !"

CHAPTER VII.

The Goat-mother arrived at home in a pitiable state of cold and exhaustion, but she was much cheered by finding the house in good order, and a warm supper awaiting her, prepared by the hands of the careful Stein-bok.

Lizbet and Lénora immediately started off with the Royal Order; which was sealed with a large crown of red sealing wax fastening down a wisp of mauve hair.

The next morning all the Goats of the neighbourhood collected in a secret cavern, where they held a patriotic meeting, and discussed their plans for the rescue and protection of the Heif-father.

Six of the strongest and most daring spirits were to start that afternoon for the Inn on the other side of the Glacier, while the rest of the Free-will corps would take it in turns to remain in ambush in the Heif-goat's garden, in case the Chamois should attempt their raid before the day they had appointed.

They all agreed that the corps should be armed to the teeth, and there was such a demand for sandpaper that the store in the Stein-bok's pack was soon exhausted.

" A rusty sword is all the deadlier, when it once gets in," said the Goat-Lieutenant. " I shan't trouble myself about petty details."

The Heif-father rescue party started to cross the Glacier

as soon as it became twilight—for they did not wish to attract attention.

The Lieutenant carried a blunderbuss, but the five privates were more lightly armed with a collection of rapiers, carving knives, daggers, spears, and sword-sticks.

Their uniforms were varied, but each wore a mauve badge on his hat, with the motto—" Goats and justice."

After half-an-hour's steady walking they reached the opposite mountain, and climbing the ladders that led to the Inn, they skirted the Châlet carefully, hiding behind the loose rocks and bushes until they were well in the shadow of the outbuildings.

" Where are you, Herr Heif?" bleated the Lieutenant in a low tone. " We are friends. You needn't be alarmed."

" In here," answered a cautious voice from one of the larger sheds. " You can't get in, though—there's no hope of breaking the door open. Iron staples and bars, and the strongest hinges. How many of you are there ?"

" Six," replied the Lieutenant. " Free-will Goats, armed to the teeth !"

" You might look at the place and see if you can find a crack anywhere," whispered the Goat-father.

The Lieutenant and his followers walked slowly round the house, examining it at every point; but it was all built of strong tree trunks tanned brown by the sunshine. Suddenly his eye lighted upon a small window. It was very high up and quite out of reach of anyone within, but the Lieutenant thought that by standing on something he might be able to raise himself sufficiently to reach it, and cut away the glass.

"Is there anything inside that *you* could stand upon ?" he enquired.

There was silence, and a sound of scuffling; then the voice of the Heif-goat : "I've been examining things, and there are two barrels. I think I could put one on the top of the other. They *might* reach to the window, but it has two great wooden bars, I couldn't break through."

"Leave that to us," said the Lieutenant, and he turned to his followers.

"Two of you get on each other's shoulders, and then *I* will be assisted up. The other three mount in the same way by my side," he said quickly. "We who are at the top will cut through the window frame with our knives, collect the glass, and drag out the Goat-father in no time."

This plan was carried out, and in spite of the unsteady position of the topmost Goats, and the uncomfortable shaking of the lower ones, the wooden bars were at length sawn through, and the glass carefully gathered together by the Lieutenant in his felt hat.

"Steady!" cried the Lieutenant, "I'm coming down in a minute, and you're beginning to shake about so, I can hardly keep my balance. Hi! Do you hear me? Steady, there!"

"I can't stand this a moment longer—my legs are giving

way beneath me!" bleated the lower Goat. " I know I
shall double up ! "

As he spoke his feet slipped from under him, and he fell
full length upon the hill-side, carrying the others with him ;
and there they all lay in a confused heap, scarcely able to
realize what had happened to them.

Fortunately, however, no one was seriously hurt. They
picked themselves up and went to work again with renewed
vigour.

"Climb up now, Herr Heif!" cried the Lieutenant. "Put
your head out, and gradually lower yourself. We'll stand
below and catch you."

" I'm a little afraid, for I know I should fall heavy! " said
the Goat-father, in a quavering voice ; but he did as he was
told, and shutting his eyes firmly, he slipped from the
window-sill and fell with a heavy *flop* into the arms waiting
to receive him.

CHAPTER VIII.

The Goat-mother had lit a comfortable fire in the Heif
Châlet, and the Goat-father's slippers were warming against
the stove ; when a sound of approaching voices and footsteps
made her start up in excited expectation.

The voices came nearer and nearer. Now she could dis-
tinguish the National Goat Song, and in another moment

the door flew open, and Herr Heif rushed in accompanied by his rescuers.

The children screamed, the Goat-mother wept tears of joy; and after a general rejoicing, the whole party sat down to a comfortable meal, during which the Lieutenant's health was drunk by the Goat-family amidst loud cheering.

"I am sorry we can't invite the whole *corps*," said the Goat-mother. "It's very cold for them outside, but the fact is I haven't sufficient crockery. As it is, I am forced to make use of oyster shells and the flower pot, though it's very much against my principles."

"Hush!" said the Goat-father, "there's someone knocking!"

There was indeed a hurried rapping at the door, and one of the Watch-Goats put in his head to say that the band of Chamois were seen advancing towards the Châlet.

The tallow candle was immediately put out, the Lieutenant and his detachment seized their weapons, and concealed themselves behind the door, and the Goat-mother and her children were shut up in an inner room, where they waited in fear and trembling.

On came the Chamois with noiseless leaps, bounding into the garden, and approaching the front door with the utmost caution. Everything appeared to be turning out according to their expectations, and they already saw themselves in imagination seated in the Heif-house, revelling in the contents of the Goat-mother's store cupboard.

Their long green coats fluttered in the air, the large

bunches of edelweiss in their hats, glistened in the moonlight. But a low, clear whistle suddenly sounded.

Each Goat sprang from his hiding place, and with a rush that took the Chamois completely by surprise, they fell upon the invaders, and drove them over the precipice.

It was a real triumph; for the Chamois flew down the mountain in the wildest confusion, falling down, and darting over each other in their hurry, and never stopping until they had reached their own haunts in the region of the distant Eismeer.

"A glorious victory!" cried the Lieutenant, "and not a drop of blood shed."

As to the Goat-mother, she had passed through such a moment of terror that she had to be assisted out of the back room by three of the guard, and revived with a cabbage leaf before she could recover herself. She then embraced everyone all round, and the Goat-father broached a barrel of lager-beer; while the tame Fox from the Inn (who had appeared at the Châlet soon after the departure of the rescue party) ran about supplying the visitors with tumblers.

The next day the Free-will Goats were disbanded, and returned to their homes; after receiving in public the thanks of the Goat-King for their distinguished behaviour, and a carved matchbox each " For valour in face of the horns of the enemy."

The Stein-bok Pedlar was begged to make his home at the

Heif Châlet, but he loved his wandering life too much to settle down.

"Keep the tame Fox instead of me, ma'am," he said, as he shook hands warmly with his friends at parting. "The poor creature is miserable in captivity."

He then made the Goat-mother a handsome present of all his remaining groceries, and departed once more upon his travels.

That same afternoon a special messenger from the Goat-King arrived with an inlaid musical chair, "as a slight token of regard," for the Heif-father.

"Well, at all events, it's better than a cuckoo clock," said the Goat-mother resignedly, "but let me warn you seriously *never to sit down upon it!* I know its ways, and though kindly meant, I should have preferred paper-knives!"

The Great Lady's Chief-Mourner.

I T was a large white house that stood on a hill. In front stretched a beautiful garden full of all kinds of rare flowers, on to which opened the windows of the sitting-rooms.

Everything was handsome and stately, and the lady who owned it was handsomer and statelier than her house.

In her velvet dress she sat under the shade of a sweeping cedar tree ; with a crowd of obsequious relations round her, trying to anticipate her lightest wishes.

"How nice it must be to be rich," thought the little kitchen-maid as she looked out through the trellis work that hid the kitchens at the side of the great house. " How happy my mistress must be. How much I should like to try just for one day what it feels like ! "—and she went back with a sigh to her work in the gloomy kitchen.

Through the latticed window she could see nothing but the paved yard, and an old tin biscuit box that stood on the window-sill, and contained two little green shoots sprouting up from the dark mould.

This little ugly box was the kitchen-maid's greatest treasure. Every day she watered it and watched over it, for she had brought the seeds from the tiny garden of her own home, and many sunny memories clustered about them. She was always looking forward to the day when the first blossoms would unfold, and now it really seemed that two buds were forming on the slender stems. The little kitchen-maid smiled with joy as she noticed them.

"I shall have flowers, too!" she said to herself hopefully.

One day, as the mistress of the house walked on the terrace by the vegetable garden, the little kitchen-maid came past suddenly with a basket of cabbages. She smiled and curtsied so prettily that the great lady nodded to her kindly, and threw her a beautiful red rose she carried in her hand.

The kitchen-maid could hardly believe her good fortune. She picked up the flower and ran with it to her bedroom, where she put it in a cracked jam-pot in water; and the whole room seemed full of its fragrance—just as the little kitchen-maid's heart was all aglow with gratitude at the kind act of the great lady.

Time passed, and the little kitchen-maid's rose withered; but the slender plants in the tin box expanded into flower, and all the yard seemed brighter for their white petals.

One day the mistress of the house fell ill. Doctors went and came, crowds of relations besieged the house, an air of gloom hung over the bright garden.

The little kitchen-maid waited anxiously for news; and

tears rolled down her face as she heard the Church bell tolling for the death of the great lady.

A grand funeral started from the white house on the hill. Carriages containing relations, who tried vainly to twist their faces into an expression of the grief they were supposed to be feeling.

Wreaths of the purest hot-house flowers covered the coffin—wreaths for which the relations had given large sums of money; but not one woven with sorrowful care by the hand of a real lover.

The sod was patted down, the dry-eyed mourners departed; and some square yards of bare earth were all that now belonged to the great lady.

When everyone had left, the little kitchen-maid crept from behind some bushes, where she had been hiding.

Her face was tear-stained, and she carried in her hand two slender white flowers.

They were the plants grown with such loving care in the old tin box on the window-sill; and she laid them with a sigh amongst the rich wreaths and crosses.

" Good-bye, dear mistress ! I have nothing else to bring you," she whispered ; and never dreamed that her gift had been the most beautiful of any—her simple love and tears.

Dame Fossie's China Dog.

RANNY PYETANGLE lived in a little thatched cottage, with a garden full of sweet-smelling, old-fashioned flowers. It was one of a long row of other thatched cottages that bordered the village street. At one end of this was the Inn, with a beautiful sign-board that creaked and swayed in the wind; at the other, Dame Fossie's shop, in which brandy-balls, ginger-snaps, balls of string, tops, cheese, tallow candles, and many other useful and entertaining things were neatly disposed in a small latticed window.

All Granny Pyetangle's relations were dead; and she lived quite alone with her little grandson 'Zekiel, who had been a mingled source of pride and worry to her, ever since he left off long-clothes and took to a short-waisted frock with a wide frill round the neck, that required constant attention in the way of washing and ironing.

'Zekiel's favourite place to play in was Granny Pyetangle's cottage doorway.

A board had been put up to prevent him rolling out on to the cobblestone pavement; and this board though very irritating to 'Zekiel in many ways—as preventing him from straying down the road and otherwise enjoying himself—was yet not to be despised, as he soon discovered, when he was learning to walk.

It was one of the few things he could grasp firmly, without its immediately sliding away, doubling up, turning head over heels, or otherwise throwing him violently down on the brick floor of the kitchen—before he knew what had happened to him!

Granny Pyetangle frequently went to have a chat with Dame Fossie, her large sun-bonnet shading her wrinkled old face, a handkerchief crossed neatly over her print bodice. On these occasions 'Zekiel accompanied his grandmother, hanging on to her skirts affectionately with one hand, whilst he waved a crust of brown bread in the other—a crust which he generally carried concealed about his person, for the two-fold purpose of assisting through his teeth and amusing himself at every convenient opportunity.

Whilst Granny Pyetangle discussed the affairs of the neighbours, 'Zekiel would sit on the floor by her side contentedly sucking his crust, and looking with awe upon the contents of the shop. Such a collection of good things seemed a perfect fairy-tale to him, and he would often settle in his own mind what he would have when he grew up and had pence to rattle about in his trousers' pocket, like Eli and Hercules Colfox.

Like most children in short petticoats, who—contrary to

K

the generally-received idea—are constantly meditating on
every subject that comes under their notice; 'Zekiel had
his own ideas about Granny Pyetangle and her friend Dame
Fossie.

His grandmother ought to have spent more of her money
on peppermint-cushions, tin trumpets, and whip-tops, and
less on those uninteresting household stores; and Dame
Fossie should have remembered that crusts are poor work
when brandy-snaps and gingerbread are spread before you,
and ought more frequently to have bestowed a biscuit on
the round-eyed 'Zekiel, as he played with the cat, or poked
pieces of stick between the cracks of the floor when Granny
Pyetangle wasn't looking.

Though 'Zekiel had no brothers and sisters, he had a great
many friends, the chief of which were Eli and Hercules
Colfox, his next door neighbours, who were very kind and
condescending to him in spite of the dignity of their
corduroy trousers.

'Zekiel had a way of ingratiating himself with everyone,
and of getting what he wanted, that inspired the slower-
witted Eli and Hercules with awe and admiration; until one
day he took it into his head to long for Dame Fossie's cele-
brated black and white spotted china dog !

All the village knew this dog, for it had stood for years
on a shelf above the collection of treasures in the shop
window. It was not an ordinary china dog such as you
can see in any china shop now-a-days, but one of the old-

fashioned kind, on which the designer had (like the early masters) expended all his art upon the dignity of expression without harassing himself with petty details.

Proudly Dame Fossie's dog looked down upon the world, sitting erect, with his golden padlock and chain glittering in any stray gleams of sunshine ; his white coat evenly spotted with black, his long drooping ears, neat row of carefully-painted black curls across the forehead, and that proud smile which, though the whole village had been smitten down before him, would still have remained unchangeable.

It was this wonderful superiority of expression that had first attracted 'Zekiel as he played about on the floor of Dame Fossie's parlour.

The china dog never looked at him with friendly good-fellowship, like the other dogs of the village. It never wanted to share his crusts, or upset him by running up against his legs just as he thought he had mastered the difficulties of " walking like Granny ! "

It was altogether a strangely attractive animal, and 'Zekiel, from the time he could first indistinctly put a name to anything, had christened it the " Fozzy-gog " out of compliment to its owner, Dame Fossie—and the " Fozzy-gog " it remained to him, and to the other children of the village, for ever after.

When 'Zekiel was nearly six years of age Granny Pye-tangle called him up to her, and asked what he would like for his birthday present.

'Zekiel sat down on a wooden stool in the chimney corner, where the iron pot hung, and meditated deeply.

" Eli and Hercules to tea, and a Fozzy-gog to play with," he said at last—and Granny Pyetangle smiled and said she would see what she could do—" 'Zekiel was a good lad, and deserved a treat."

'Zekiel's birthday arrived, and the moment he opened his eyes he saw that his grandmother had redeemed her promise.

On a rush chair beside his pillow stood the very double of the Fozzy-gog !—yellow eyes, gold collar and padlock, black spots, and all complete !

'Zekiel sprang up, and scrambled into his clothes as quickly as possible. He danced round Granny Pyetangle in an ecstasy of delight, and scarcely eat any breakfast, he was in such a hurry to show his treasure to his two friends.

As he handed it over the low hedge that separated the two gardens he felt a proud boy, but Eli did not appear so enthusiastic as 'Zekiel expected. He said that "chaney dogs was more for Grannies nor for lads," and that if he had been in 'Zekiel's place he would have chosen a fine peg-top.

Poor 'Zekiel was disappointed. The tears gathered in his eyes. He hugged the despised china dog fondly to him, and carried it indoors to put in a place of honour in Granny Pyetangle's oak corner-cupboard—where it looked out proudly from behind the glass doors, in company with the best tea-cups, a shepherdess tending a woolly lamb, two greyhounds on stony-white cushions, and Grandfather Pyetangle's horn snuff-box.

Time passed on, and 'Zekiel's petticoats gave place to corduroy breeches, but his devotion to the china dog never waned. He would talk to it, and tell it all his plans and fancies, and several times he almost persuaded himself that it wagged its tail and nodded to him. In fact, he was quite sure that when Granny Pyetangle was ill that winter, the china dog was conscious of the fact, and looked at him with its yellow eyes full of compassion and sympathy.

Poor Granny Pyetangle was certainly very ill. She had suffered from rheumatism for many years, and was sometimes almost bent double with it ; but that autumn it came on with increased violence, and 'Zekiel, who nursed his old grandmother devotedly, had to sit by the bed-side for hours giving her medicine, or the food a neighbour prepared for her, just as she required it.

Granny Pyetangle was sometimes rather cross in those days, and would scold poor 'Zekiel for "clumping in his boots" and "worritting"—but 'Zekiel was very patient.

"Sick people *is* wearing at times," said Dame Fossie. "Come you down to me sometimes, 'Zekiel, and I'll let you play with my chaney dog. It isn't fit as young lads should be cooped up always ! "—and when Granny Pyetangle had a neighbour with her, 'Zekiel gladly obeyed.

One evening he ran down the village street with a smile on his face, and a new penny in his pocket. Squire Hancock had given it to him for holding his horse, and he was going to spend it at Dame Fossie's on a cake for his grandmother.

Twilight was falling, yet Dame Fossie's shop was not lighted up; which was strange, as a little oil lamp generally burned in the window as soon as it grew dusk.

The shop door was shut and locked, and 'Zekiel ran round to the back, and climbing on the edge of the rain-water butt, he peered over the white dimity blind, into the silent kitchen.

No one was there, and yet Dame Fossie must be some-where in the house, for he distinctly heard sounds of thumping and scraping going on upstairs.

"I'll get in through the window, and surprise her!" said 'Zekiel; and as one of the latticed panes was unfastened he proceeded to push it gently open, and creep in on to the table that stood just beneath it.

He unlatched the kitchen door, and stole up the ricketty staircase.

The sounds continued, but more loudly. Evidently there was a house-cleaning going on, and 'Zekiel supposed this was why Dame Fossie had been deaf to his repeated knockings. He lifted the latch of the room from which the noise proceeded, and peeping cautiously in, beheld such a strange sight that he remained rooted to the ground with astonishment.

Dame Fossie's furniture was piled up in one corner—the oak bureau, and the rush-bottomed chairs, inside the four-post bedstead. A pail of water stood in the middle of the floor; and close by was the Fozzy-gog himself, with a mop between his paws, working away with the greatest energy.

He was about four times his ordinary size, as upright as 'Zekiel himself, and was directing the work of several other china dogs; amongst whom 'Zekiel immediately recognized his own property, Granny Pyetangle's birthday present!

Everyone seemed to be too busy to notice 'Zekiel as he stood half in the doorway. Two of the dogs were scouring the floor with a pair of Dame Fossie's best scrubbing brushes, another was dusting the ceiling with a feather broom; whilst several, seated round the four-post bedstead, were polishing it with bees' wax and "elbow-grease." They all listened to the Fozzy-gog with respectful attention, as he issued his directions; for he was evidently a person in authority.

It did not occur to 'Zekiel to be surprised that all the dogs were chatting together in very comprehensible Dorsetshire English. To see them actually living, and moving about, was such an extraordinary thing that it swallowed up every other feeling, even that of fear.

"Make haste, my good dogs! Put the furniture straight, and have all ready. Dame Fossie will be returning soon, and we must be back on our shelves before her key turns," said the Fozzie-gog cheerfully.

The dogs all worked with renewed energy, and before 'Zekiel could collect his scattered wits enough to retreat or hide himself, the room was in perfect order, and out trooped the china dogs carrying the buckets, brooms, and brushes, they had been using.

As they caught sight of 'Zekiel, the Fozzie-gog jumped several feet into the air.

" What! 'Zekiel spying upon us ! " he screamed angrily. " Bring the lad into the kitchen. We must examine into this," and he clattered down the steep stairs with his mop into the wash-house.

Poor 'Zekiel followed trembling. His own dog had crept up to him, and slipped one paw into his hand, whispering hurriedly, " Don't be downhearted, 'Zekiel. Never contradict him, and he will forgive you in a year or two ! "

" A year or two ! " thought 'Zekiel wretchedly. " And never contradict him, indeed! when he says I was spying on him. A likely thing ! " and he clung to his friend, and dragged him in with him into the kitchen.

The Fozzy-gog sat in Dame Fossie's high-backed chair in the chimney corner, the other china dogs grouped around him. It reminded 'Zekiel of the stories of Kings and their Courts, and no doubt the Fozzy-gog *was* a king—in his own opinion at least.

He questioned 'Zekiel minutely as to how he happened to come there so late in the evening ; and to all the questions 'Zekiel answered most truthfully.

The frown on the Fozzy-gog's face relaxed more and more—an amiable smile began to curl the corners of his mouth, and he extended his paw in a dignified manner towards 'Zekiel, who felt like a prisoner reprieved.

" We forgive you, 'Zekiel! You have always been a good friend to us, and your own dog speaks well of you," said the Fozzy-gog benignly. " You must give us your word you will never mention what you have seen. In the future we must be china dogs to you, and *nothing more ;* but in return for this you may ask one thing of us, and, if possible, we will grant it."

'Zekiel hesitated. Wild possibilities of delight in the shape of ponies and carts flitted rapidly through his mind, and then the remembrance of Granny Pyetangle, lying ill and suffering on her bed in the little sloping attic, drove everything else from his mind.

" I want my poor old Granny to be well again," he said, looking the Fozzy-gog bravely in the face—" and I don't want naught else. If you'll do that, I'll promise anything —that's to say, anything in reason," added 'Zekiel, who prided himself on this diplomatic finish to his sentence— which was one he had frequently heard his grandmother make use of in moments of state and ceremony.

The Fozzy-gog appeared to be favourably impressed by 'Zekiel's request. He rose from his chair, and waved his paw graciously.

" We dismiss this gathering! " he cried. " And you, Pyetangle "—pointing to 'Zekiel's china dog—" take your master home, and bring him to our meeting at the cross-

roads to-morrow at midnight. Do not fail. Farewell!"
As he spoke the Fozzy-gog shrank and stiffened. His
black curls acquired their usual glaze, and he had just time
to jump upon the shelf above the shop window, before he
froze into his immovable china self again.

The other dogs disappeared through the open kitchen
casement; and 'Zekiel found himself in the village street
without in the least knowing how he got there!

It was almost dark as he ran home, but as he swung open
the garden gate, he fancied he saw something white standing
exactly in the centre of the pathway. He was sure he
heard a faint barking, and a voice whispered—" Wait a
minute, 'Zekiel, I want to talk to you." 'Zekiel retreated a
step, and sat down gasping on a flower bed.

" I want to talk to you," repeated the little voice.

'Zekiel craned forward, though he was trembling with
fright, and saw in the fast gathering shadows his own china
dog, standing beside Granny Pyetangle's favourite lavender
bush—though how it managed to get there so quickly he
could not imagine! He stretched out his hand to stroke
it, and started up, as instead of the cold china, he felt the
soft curls of a fluffy fur coat.

" Tell me what it all means! Oh, do'ee, now!" said
'Zekiel, almost crying.

The china dog sat down by 'Zekiel's side, and putting one
paw affectionately on his knee, looked up in his face, with
his honest yellow eyes.

"The Fozzy-gog has commissioned me to explain all about it," he said confidentially. "So don't be frightened, and no harm will come of it! Twice every month (if we can escape unobserved) we take the form of ordinary dogs, and meet together to amuse ourselves, or to work for our owners. There are many of us in the village, and as the Fozzy-gog is our ruler, we are bound to obey him, and to work more for old Dame Fossie than for anybody else. Yesterday we knew she was going to visit her married daughter. We determined to have a thorough house-cleaning, and were just in the midst of it when you came in! It was a good thing the Fozzy-gog happened to be in a good temper, and knew you well! We have never before been discovered. He is a hasty temper, and it certainly *was* irritating!"

'Zekiel began to recover from his terror, and grasped the china dog by the paw. He felt proud to think that his ideas about china dogs had proved true. They were not merely "chaney"—as Eli and Hercules contemptuously expressed it; but were really as much alive as he was himself, after all!

"However did you manage to get out of Granny Pye-tangle's cupboard?" enquired 'Zekiel, curiously.

"Oh, I put those lazy greyhounds and the shepherdess at it," replied the china dog. "They worked all night, and managed to undo the latch early this afternoon. They're bound to work for me like all the inferior china things," and he shook his head superciliously.

" And now," said 'Zekiel, " please tell me how the Fozzy-gog is going to get my Granny well."

" Ah, that I mayn't tell you," said the china dog. "You must come with me to-morrow night to the Dog-wood, and you will hear all about it."

As he spoke, he began to shrink and stiffen in the same remarkable way as the Fozzy-gog, and a moment after he was standing in his ordinary shape in the centre of the cobblestone pathway.

The moonlight shone upon his quaint little figure and the golden padlock at his neck. 'Zekiel sprang up just as the cottage door opened, and a neighbour came out calling, "'Zekiel ! 'Zekiel ! Drat the lad ! Where be you gone to ? "

'Zekiel tucked the china dog under his arm and hurried in, receiving a good scolding from Granny Pyetangle and her friend for " loitering," but he felt so light-hearted and cheerful, the hard words fell round him quite harmlessly.

"Granny 'll be well to-morrow! Granny 'll be well to-morrow!" he kept repeating to himself over and over again, and he ran into the kitchen just before going to bed to make sure the things in the corner cupboard were safely shut away for the night.

'Zekiel hardly knew how he got through the next day, so impatient was he for the evening. Granny Pyetangle was certainly worse. The neighbours came in and shook their heads sadly over her, and Dame Fossie hobbled up from her shop and offered to spend the night there, as it was

" no' fit for young lads to have such responsibilities "—and this offer 'Zekiel eagerly accepted.

As soon as it grew dusk, he unlatched the door of the oak cupboard; and then being very tired—for he had worked hard since daylight—he sat down in Granny Pyetangle's large chair, and in a minute was fast asleep.

He was awakened by a series of pulls at his smock-frock; and starting up he saw that it was quite dark, except for the glow of a few ashes on the hearth-stone, and that the china dog, grown to the same size as he had been the evening before, was trying to arouse him.

" Wake up, 'Zekiel! " he said in a low voice. " Dame Fossie is upstairs with your Granny, and we must be off."

'Zekiel rubbed his eyes, and taking his cap down from a peg, and tying a check comforter round his neck, he followed the china dog from the kitchen, and closed and latched the door behind him.

Out in the moonlit street, the china dog kept as much as possible in the shadow of the houses; 'Zekiel following, his hob-nailed boots *click, clicking* against the rough stones as he stumbled sleepily along.

They soon left the village behind them, and plunged into a wood, which, stretching for miles across hill and dale, was known to be a favourite haunt of smugglers.

'Zekiel instantly became very wide awake indeed, and unpleasant cold shivers ran down his back, as he thought he saw black and white forms gliding amongst the trees, and yellow eyes glancing at him between the bare branches.

" It isn't smugglers.   It's the dogs galloping to the meeting place," said the china dog, who seemed able to read 'Zekiel's thoughts in a very unnatural manner.

They soon left the rough pathway they had been following, and 'Zekiel, clinging to the china dog's paw, found himself in the densest part of the wood, which was only dimly lighted by a few scattered moonbeams.

" We are getting near the Dog-wood now," said the china dog as they hurried on, and in another moment they came out on to the middle of a clearing, round which a dense thicket of red-stemmed dog-wood bushes grew in the greatest luxuriance.

In the centre was a large square stone, like a stand ; on which sat the Fozzy-gog, surrounded by about fifty china dogs of all shapes and sizes, but each one with a gold padlock and chain round his neck, without which none were admitted to the secret society of the " Fozzy-gogs."

'Zekiel was drawn reluctantly into the magic circle, while every dog wagged his tail as a sign of friendly greeting.

The Fozzy-gog nodded graciously, and immediately the dogs commenced a wild dance, with many leaps and bounds ; round the stone on which their ruler was seated.

The moonlight shone brightly on their glancing white coats ; and behind rustled the great oak trees, their boughs twisted into fantastic forms, amidst which the wind whistled eerily.

'Zekiel shuddered as he looked at the strange scene, and longed sincerely to be back again in his little bed at Granny Pyetangle's.

" However, it won't do to show I'm afraid, or don't like it," he said to himself, so he capered and hopped with the others until he was quite giddy and exhausted, and forced to sit down on a grassy bank to recover himself.

" The trees are playing very well to-night," said a dog as he skipped by. " Come and have another dance ? " and he flew round and round like a humming top.

'Zekiel shook his head several times. He was so out of breath he could only gasp hurriedly—" No, no ! No more, thank you ! " but his friend had already disappeared.

The Fozzy-gog now approached him. He carried something in his paw, which he placed in 'Zekiel's hand.

" Put this on Grandmother Pyetangle's forehead when you return to-night—promise that you will keep silence for ever about what you have seen—and to-morrow she will be well ! "

" I promise," said 'Zekiel. " Oh, Fozzy-gog ! I'll never forget it ! "

" No thanks," said the Fozzy-gog. " I like deeds more than words. Pyetangle shall take you home."

He beckoned to 'Zekiel's dog, who came up rather sulkily—and 'Zekiel found himself outside the magic circle, and well on his way home, almost before he could realize that they had started !

As he entered Granny Pyetangle's little garden, he saw that a light was still burning in her attic.

He went softly into the kitchen. It was quite dark, but a ray of moonlight enabled him to see the china dog open the cupboard ; and, rapidly shrinking, place himself on his proper shelf again.

'Zekiel then took off his boots, ran up the creaking stairs, and tapped softly at Granny Pyetangle's bedroom. No one answered, so he pushed open the door.

Dame Fossie sat sleeping peacefully in a large rush-bottomed chair by the fireplace—and Granny Pyetangle, on her bed under the chintz curtains, was sleeping too.

'Zekiel laid the Fozzy-gog's leaf carefully on her forehead, and creeping from the room, threw himself on his own little bed, and was soon as fast asleep as the two old women.

The next morning, when Granny Pyetangle awoke, she said she felt considerably better, and so energetic was she that Dame Fossie had great difficulty in persuading her not to get up.

Dame Fossie tidied up the place, and was much annoyed to find a dead leaf sticking to Granny Pyetangle's scanty grey hair. " How a rubbishy leaf o' dog-wood came to get there, is more nor *I* can account for," she said crossly, as she swept it away into the fire, before 'Zekiel could interfere to rescue it.

Granny Pyetangle's recovery was wonderfully rapid. Every day she was able to do a little more, and 'Zekiel's triumph was complete when he was allowed to help her down the stairs into the kitchen, and seat her quavering, but happy, on the great chair in the chimney corner.

" Well, it do seem pleasant to be about agin," said Granny Pyetangle, smoothing her white linen apron. " No'but you have kept the place clean, 'Zekiel, like a good lad. There's those things in corner cupboard as bright as chaney can be ! and that chaney dog o' yours sitting as life-like as you please ! It wouldn't want much fancy to say he was wagging his tail and looking at me quite welcoming ! "

The wood fire blazed and crackled, the kettle sang on its chain in the wide chimney. Granny Pyetangle was almost well, and quite happy; and 'Zekiel felt his heart overflowing with gratitude towards the Fozzy-gog.

" I'll never forget him. Never ! " said 'Zekiel to himself, " and I wouldn't tell upon him not if anyone was to worrit me ever so ! "—and indeed he never did.

Years passed, and Dame Fossie's shop was shut, and Dame Fossie herself was laid to rest. Her daughter inherited most of her possessions; but—" to my young friend 'Zekiel Pyetangle, I will and bequeath my china dog, hoping as he'll be a kind friend to it," stood at the end of the sheet of paper which did duty as her will. And so 'Zekiel became the owner of the Fozzy-gog after all !

Granny Pyetangle has long since passed away, but the little thatched cottage is still there, with the garden full of lavender bushes and sweet-smelling flowers. From the glass

L

door of the corner cupboard the Fozzy-gog and his companion
look out upon the world with the same inscrutable expression ; and 'Zekiel himself, old and decrepit, but still cheerful,
may at this moment be sitting in the cottage porch, watching
his little grandchildren play about the cobblestone pathway,
or talking over old times with Eli and Hercules Colfox, who,
hobbling in for a chat, take a pull at their long pipes, and
bemoan the inferiority of everything that does not belong to
the time when " us were all lads together."

Princess Sidigunda's Golden Shoes.

PRINCESS SIDIGUNDA lived with her parents in a beautiful old castle by the sea. It was so near that the royal gardens sloped down gradually to the shore, and from its battlements—where the little Princess was allowed to walk sometimes on half-holidays—she could watch the ships with their gaily-painted prows and golden dragons' heads, sweeping over the water in quest of new lands and fresh adventures.

Princess Sidigunda was an only child, and at her christening every gift you can imagine had been showered upon her.

The Trolls of the Woods gave her beauty ; the Trolls of the Water, a free, bright spirit ; the Mountain-Trolls, good health ; and last, but not least, her chief Godfather, the Troll of the Seashore, had given her a beautiful little pair of golden slippers.

"Never let the child take them off her feet," said the old Troll. "As long as she keeps them she will be happy. If ever they are lost the Princess's troubles will begin."

"But they will grow too small for her!" said the Queen anxiously.

"Oh no, they won't!" said the old Troll. "They will grow as she grows, so you needn't trouble about that."

Time went on, and the little Princess grew to be ten years old.

The old Troll's promise was fulfilled, and her life had been a perfectly happy one. Watched by her faithful nurse, she had never had any opportunity of losing her magic shoes;

and though she often bathed and played about the shore with her young companions, she was never allowed to be without one of her attendants, in case she should forget her Godfather's caution.

One fine summer afternoon, the Princess, with some of her friends, ran down to the sands from the little gate in the castle wall.

The sea looked green and beautiful, light waves curling over on the narrow strip of yellow shore.

"Let's wade!" cried the Princess. "My nurse is ill in bed, and my two ladies think we are playing in the garden. We'll have a little treat of being alone, and enjoy ourselves!"

"We must take our slippers off," said one of the children, as they raced along.

"Oh, I wish *I* could!" cried the Princess. "I don't believe *once* would matter. I'll put them in a safe place where the sea can't get at them," and as she spoke she pulled off her golden shoes, and hid them in a great hurry behind a sand-bank.

The Princess's little friends ran off laughing; while she followed, her hair streaming, her bare feet twinkling in the sunlight.

"How nice it is to be free, without those tiresome shoes!" cried the Princess.

The children paddled in the water until they were tired, and then Sidigunda thought it was time to put on her slippers again. She ran to the bank, but gave a cry of astonishment—she could only find one of her golden shoes! Tears sprang to her eyes as she looked about her wildly.

"Oh what shall I do?" she cried. "My shoe! My Godfather's shoe!"

The children gathered round her eagerly.

"It must be there. Who can have taken it?"

They searched the low sand dunes up and down, but not a trace of the lost slipper could be found. It was gone as entirely as if it had never existed; and as the Princess drew on the remaining one, the tears rolled down her face, and fell upon the sand-hill by which she was sitting.

"Oh, Godfather! dear Godfather! come and help me!" she wailed. "Do come and help me!"

At her cry, the sand-hill began to quiver and shake strangely. It heaved up, and an old man's head, with a long grey beard, appeared in the middle; followed slowly by a little brown-coated body.

"What is the matter, God-daughter? Your tears trickled down to me and woke me up, just as I was comfortably sleeping," he said querulously. "They're salter than the sea, and I can't stand them."

"My shoe's gone! Oh! whatever am I to do? I'm *so* sorry, Godfather!"

"So you ought to be!" said the old man sharply. "I told you something bad would happen if you ever took them off. The question is now, Where's the shoe gone to?"

He leant his elbows on the mound, and looked out to sea.

"Just what I thought!" he exclaimed. "The Sea-children have taken it for a boat. I *must* speak to the Sea-grandmother about them, and get her to keep them in better order."

"Oh, it's gone then, and I shall never get it back again!" wept the Princess. "What am I to do, Godfather?"

"Have you courage enough to go and find your shoe by yourself?"

"If that's the only way to get it back," said the Princess bravely.

"Well, then, you must start immediately, or the Sea-

children will have hidden it away somewhere. You will be
obliged to have a passport, but I'll tell you how to get that.
Take this veil"—and he drew a thin, transparent piece of
silvery gauze from his pocket—" and throw it over your head
whenever you go under the water. With it you will be able
to breathe and see, as well as if you were on dry land. From
this flask "—and he handed Sidigunda a curious little gold
bottle—"you must pour a few drops on to your remaining
shoe, and whenever you do so it will change in a moment
into a boat, a horse, or a fish, as you desire it."

"How am I to start, and where am I to go to?" asked
the Princess, trying not to feel frightened at the prospect
before her.

"Launch your shoe as a boat, and float on till you meet
the Sea-Troll, who is an old friend of mine. Explain your
errand to him, and say I begged him to direct you and give
you a passport. And now one last word before I leave you.
Never, *whatever* happens, cry again; for there is nothing
worries me so much, and I want to finish my sleep
comfortably."

With these words the old Troll collected his long grey
beard which had strayed over the sand-hill; and folding it
round him, he disappeared in the hole again.

Princess Sidigunda did not give herself time to think.
She ran down to the edge of the water, took off her golden
shoe, and poured some of the contents of her Godfather's
flask over it.

It changed immediately into a boat, into which the Princess stepped tremblingly; and it floated away over the blue water until the little Princess, straining her eyes eagerly, lost sight of her home, and the land faded away into a mere streak upon the horizon.

"I wonder when I shall meet the Sea-Troll and what he's like," thought Princess Sidigunda. "I suppose I shall be able to recognize him somehow."

As she thought this, she noticed that some object was rapidly floating towards her. It did not look like a boat, and as it came nearer and nearer, she could see that it was a large shell, on which an old man with a long beard was seated cross-legged, surrounded by a crowd of laughing Sea-children. They clung to the sides of the shell, swum round it, or climbed up to rest themselves on its crinkled edges.

"Who are you, and what are you doing here?" cried the old man in a gruff voice.

The Princess trembled; but she seized her veil and the little flask, and holding them out she repeated her God-father's message.

"I'll see what I can do, though really these children wear me out!" said the Sea-Troll. "I can't keep my eye on all of them at once! You had better go down to the Sea-city, and ask if they've carried your shoe there. If not, the Troll-writers will tell you where it is. Show this to the city guard, and they will direct you to the Palace." He gave the

Princess a flat shell on which some letters were engraved. "Sink down at once," he continued; "you are over the city now," and with a wave of his hand he sailed away with the children, and was soon out of sight.

"I suppose there's nothing else to be done," sighed Sidigunda, and throwing the scarf over her head, she poured a few drops from the bottle upon her shoe.

"Turn into a fish and carry me down to the Sea-city!" she said.

In a moment she felt herself sinking through the clear water, deeper and deeper, with a delicious drowsy feeling that almost soothed her to sleep. She knew she was *not* asleep though, for she could see the misty forms of sea creatures, darting about in the dim shadows, and great waving sea-weeds—crimson, yellow, and brown—floating up from the rippled sand beneath.

And now the shoe swum straight on, darting through the water like an eel; until a large town came in sight, with high walls and Palaces, and shining domes covered with mother-o'-pearl.

They stopped at a great gate, before which a fish dressed as a sentry was standing.

As soon as he saw the little Princess, he drew his sword, and came gliding towards her.

"Your name and business!" he enquired, in a high thin voice.

"I am Princess Sidigunda, seeking my golden shoe, and I bring this from the Sea-Troll," said the Princess coura-

geously. " Will you tell me where I am to find the Trolls
of the Palace ? "

The fish handed the shell back sulkily, and pointed up
the street.

" Go straight through till you come to the marble building
with the pearls over the door," he said ; and gave the Princess
a poke with the handle of his sword, that pushed her through
the gate, almost before she had time to draw on her golden
shoe again.

" What a rude, ill-bred sentry ! " said Sidigunda.   " My
father would be very angry if any of *our* soldiers behaved
so ; but then, of course, this one is only a fish.   What a
strange country I seem to have got into ! "

She walked along the street, looking on each side of her
curiously.

Many of the houses had transparent domes, like beautiful
soap bubbles ; some were built of coloured pebbles, and pink
and red coral, with branching trees of green and brown
seaweed growing up, beside and over them.

Everything was strange, and unlike the earth ; but what
struck the Princess most was that no inhabitants were to
be seen anywhere.   A few fish swam about lazily, otherwise
an unbroken silence reigned in the Sea-city.

Far away, at the end of the wide sanded road, a great
marble palace towered over the surrounding houses ; and as
the Princess neared it she saw that the doors were wide
open.   She walked in fearlessly, and found herself in a large

hall, with walls entirely covered with cockle-shells. Long stone tables filled the middle of the room; at which a crowd of small brown-coated men were seated, scribbling away with long pens, but in total silence.

The great grey beards of some of the writers had touched the ground, and even twisted themselves round the legs of the benches on which the old men were sitting.

Princess Sidigunda stood for a minute looking on, curiously. She then went up to one of the Trolls and pulled him gently by the sleeve.

He did not look up, but his pen slightly slackened its speed.

"What do you want?" he enquired in an uninterested voice. "Make haste, for I have no time to spare!"

"What rude people they all are!" thought the Princess. "The Sea-Troll said you would tell me how to find my golden shoe," she continued aloud.

"I wish the Sea-Troll would mind his own business!" said the little brown man vindictively. "He's always distracting us from our State business with all sorts of messages."

"Are you working for the State?" enquired Sidigunda.

"Of course! I thought every oyster knew that," replied the brown Troll.

"Are they particularly uneducated, then?" asked the Princess.

"Why they're *babies!*" said the brown Troll. "You can

see them any day in their beds by the side of the road, if you
have eyes in your head."

" What a place to keep babies in ! " thought the Princess,
but she said nothing, for she saw that the old Troll's dis-
position was very irritable.

" Would you tell me one thing," she began. " I do so
much want to know why I saw no one in the streets as I
came along. Where have all the people gone to ? "

" Well, of *all* the idi——" commenced the brown Troll,
then checked himself with an effort. " Of course you can't
know how foolish your questions sound," he said. " When
you're two or three hundred years old I daresay you'll be
more sensible. Why all the people are asleep—you don't
suppose it's the same as in *your* country ! "

" Do they sleep all the time ? " asked the Princess.

" Not all the time, of course. In this town it's two weeks
at a stretch. In other places more, or less. By this arrangement we always have half the population asleep, and half
awake—much pleasanter and less crowding. I can't think
why it's not done in other places ! "

Princess Sidigunda looked surprised.

" Will the children who took my shoe be asleep ? " she
enquired anxiously.

" Not they ! " said the brown Troll crossly, " I wish
they would be ! Children under twelve *never* sleep.
It's like having a crowd of live eels always round me !
I'd put them to sleep when they were a month old, and not

let them wake till they came of age, if I had *my* way!"

The Princess felt rather frightened of this savage little brown man. She was afraid to ask any more questions, though she longed to know why he and his companions were not asleep too.

" Go straight down the street," commenced the old Troll abruptly, "out of the green gate, along the road to the open country. Turn your shoe into a horse, and don't stop till you reach the Crab-boy's hut. He will direct you."

" That sounds simple enough," thought the Princess, " but I wish he would tell me a little more ! "

The brown Troll, however, refused to open his mouth again, and Princess Sidigunda was obliged to start off upon her wanderings, with no more guide than the few words he had chosen to speak to her.

She ran down the silent street, and out at the green gate ; the Fish-sentry allowing her to pass without objection. As soon as she reached the country road, she walked more slowly. She particularly wanted to see the beds with the Sea-babies, which the old Troll had spoken about.

For some distance she noticed nothing except wide sandy plains dotted with rocks, shells, and waving forests of giant seaweed—huge fish darting about in all directions—but at last the scenery grew wilder ; and close to the road side she came upon a grove of oysters, each half-open shell containing a Sea-child, whose head and arms appeared above the edges of the shell, while its feet and body were invisible.

Beside them sat an old woman, grey and wrinkled; with a small switch in her hand, with which she occasionally touched the Sea-babies as they leaned too far from their shells, or as their laughter rose too noisily.

The little Princess stopped and looked at the children curiously; and the old woman stepped forward and made a polite curtsey.

"They are rather noisy to-day," she said deprecatingly. "The oyster-nurses have gone out for a holiday, and I have to keep the whole bed in order!"

"I should like to wait and play with them," said the Princess, "but I really am in such a hurry—I've lost my golden shoe."

"Oh, you're going to the Crab-boy, I suppose?" said the old woman. "Down the road as straight as you can go, and you'll come to his hut," and she turned away to the children again.

Sidigunda took off her slipper, and poured out some drops from her magic bottle.

Immediately it grew larger and larger; and she had just time to spring in, before it galloped away with a series of bounds that made it very difficult to cling on.

Faster and faster it went, until the country seemed only a flying haze; and just as the Princess began to feel she could endure no more, it stopped abruptly before a small hut.

Outside the door a boy sat on a stone seat, playing on a

long horn whose notes echoed among the rocky hills that surrounded him.

Princess Sidigunda looked at the boy with a friendly smile. He stopped playing, and made room for her to sit down beside him.

" I knew you were coming," he said. " You want to go to the Sea-grandmother, don't you ? "

" Yes, I do!" said the Princess. "Do you live here all alone ? "

" Why, of course," replied the Crab-herd, " I look after all the crabs of the district. You may see me collect them if you like, for if I'm to go with you now, I must shut them up safely before starting."

As he said this, he rose, and blowing a few notes on his horn, he walked slowly along, followed by the Princess.

As the horn sounded ; crabs of every size and colour came darting out from the stones, and scuttled across the sand towards the Crab-boy. There were red and green, yellow and brown, large and small—a procession growing larger and larger, until it reached an enclosed space, into which the boy guided it, and then shut the gate securely.

The Princess had dropped down to rest upon a conch-shell, in the shade of some purple sea-weed, and she looked up at the Crab-herd with her large blue eyes, while he counted his crabs, and chased in one or two of the stragglers.

" Is the Sea-grandmother's house far off ? " she asked thoughtfully.

"Up in the great mountains, no distance from here. She lives in a cave, with plenty of space for her knitting."

"Does she knit *much*?" enquired Sidigunda.

"Yes: she knits and spins too. She never leaves off; and never has for hundreds and thousands of years."

"What a very old lady she must be! Old enough to be a great-great-great-grandmother!" cried the Princess in astonishment.

"If you said three hundred '*greats*' you would be nearer the real thing," remarked the Crab-boy. "But come now, follow me, and we will start immediately."

Princess Sidigunda got up, and taking the Crab-herd's hand, they set off down the road towards the mountains.

As they reached the foot of the grey cliffs, the Crab-boy unfolded a pair of fin-like wings from his elbows, and began to swim upwards—leaving the little Princess with her arms stretched out imploringly towards him.

"Oh, *don't* leave me here by myself!" she cried. "I shall never find my way to the Sea-grandmother!"

"Why there she is, just above us in that cave in the side of the mountain," said the Crab-boy. "Don't you see her beautiful white hair, and the flash of her knitting-needles?"

The Princess looked up, and there sat a beautiful old lady in a hole in the rock, high, high above them. A crowd of Sea-children played about her, and seemed to be carrying away the cloud-like white knitting as fast as it flowed from her busy fingers.

M

She bent her head towards Sidigunda, and nodded to her, without ceasing her work for a moment.

"Come, Princess, and talk to me!" she called in a sweet, low voice. "Take your shoe off, and it will bring you here in a moment."

Sidigunda did as she was told—for the old lady spoke as if she were used to being obeyed without question—and found herself floating upwards, until she alighted on a broad ledge right in front of the Sea-grandmother.

"So you have come all this way to find your golden shoe?" the old lady said in her clear, even voice. "Sit down, and tell me all about it."

The Princess thought the Sea-grandmother's face young and lovely. It was smooth and unwrinkled; eyes clear as crystal, with blue depths in them, shining out with a soft benign look; while her slim hands turned and twisted unceasingly, and her long green dress fell round her in wave-like folds.

Her smile was so soft and kind, that the Princess felt as if she had known her all her life.

"I have sent for your shoe, my child," she said. "Those tiresome grandchildren of mine give me a great deal of trouble. I can't keep my eyes on all of them at once, and so they are always in mischief!"

Sidigunda looked up in the gentle face; and sat down confidingly beside the Sea-grandmother.

"Do you always knit so busily, Grandmother?" she said,

as she watched the white foamy fabric float off the needles.

" Of course, child. I have been working like this for thousands and thousands of years. Who do you imagine would provide the waves with nightcaps if *I* ever stopped ? When the wind blows and they dance, or when they curl over on the shore, they would be cold indeed, without my comfortable white nightcaps ! "

" Can you get me my shoe, dear Grandmother ? " asked the little Princess wistfully.

" Certainly, dear child. Though if you had not come at once, you might have had to wait a few hundred years or so, before I could have found it for you. The children wander so far now-a-days ! Have you seen it ? " the Sea-grand-mother continued, turning to some of the children who surrounded her.

" Oh, yes," they answered in chorus. " Just now it floated above us. We can fetch it in a minute ! "

" Swim away then, as fast as you can ! " cried the Sea-grandmother, and the children darted off like fish through the green clearness of the water.

The sound of their laughter had hardly died away in the distance, before they reappeared, dragging the golden shoe behind them ; and the Princess, with smiles of joy, embraced them all as she drew it on to her foot again.

" Oh, thank you, dearest Grandmother ! I don't know how I can show you how grateful I am," cried Sidigunda.

" By going home at once to your father and mother, and

by promising me *never* again to be disobedient," said the
Sea-grandmother gravely. " Give me your shoe, and I will
order it to take you back to the Castle."

She stopped her needles for a moment, and passed her
hand over the slipper : then kissed the little Princess, and
waved the knitting rapidly before her.

A white cloud seemed to float over Sidigunda, and she
felt herself lifted up with a soothing motion, until on opening
her eyes she found she was once more in the region of the
fresh air and sunshine. Looking round, she saw the ruffled
surface of the sea, and the waves breaking upon the shore
before the Castle.

Her heart beat with happiness, as the golden shoe landed
her safely on the beach ; and she ran up through the little
gate into the Castle gardens, right into the arms of her
mother, who was pacing up and down with her attendants,
in great anxiety.

Under the shade of some spreading fir trees the Princess
related her adventures, begging the King and Queen to
forgive her for her disobedience ; and the whole Court was
so delighted at her return that everyone forgot to scold her.

That evening bonfires were lighted on all the hill-tops ;
and a great banquet was held in the Castle, at which the
Princess appeared amidst loud cheering, and, holding her
father's hand, drank from a golden goblet to the health of
her Godfather, the Shore-Troll, and the Sea-grandmother.

𝔗𝔥𝔢 𝔅𝔞𝔡𝔤𝔢𝔯'𝔰 𝔖𝔠𝔥𝔬𝔬𝔩,

OR,

THE ADVENTURES OF A BEAR FAMILY.

CHAPTER I.

N the very heart of a great forest in Sweden lived a Bear family, called " Bjornson."

They were much respected throughout the whole neighbourhood, for they were kind and hospitable to everyone ; and as their home was in such an unfrequented part of the country they were able often to give entertainments which it was quite safe to attend without fear of Foresters or other human inconveniences.

Their house was built of large stones, neatly roofed with pine branches, and was reached by a winding path through the rocks, the entrance to which had become covered by a dense thicket of bushes. A small wire had been cunningly arranged by the Bear-father, so that in the event of any stranger entering the door a bell would be rung in the Bear-kitchen ; but so far the household had fortunately never been alarmed by this contrivance.

The two Bjornson children, Knut and Otto, led a very happy life in the forest. Whenever they liked they could bring some of their young companions home from the School-house in the evening; and then the Bear-mother would seat herself on a tree-stump and play tunes for them to dance to—for Fru Bjornson was highly educated, and had learnt the concertina in all its branches.

This of course was all very delightful : but every morning Knut and Otto were obliged to start off at daybreak with their books and satchels for the forest School, and there a time of trouble usually awaited them. It was kept by an old Badger of very uncertain temper, and all his pupils stood in great awe of the birch rod which lay in a conspicuous place upon his writing-table.

" It's all very well for the Hedgehogs," the scholars often grumbled to each other. " Of course *they* can do just what they like, as they happen to be covered all over with quills— but for *us* it's a very different affair ! "

Certainly strict discipline was maintained by the Badger during School time. His eyes seemed to be upon everyone at once, and it was vain to try and crack nuts, draw carica-tures, or eat peppermint lozenges—the rod would come down immediately with a *thump !* and the offender, as he stood in a corner of the room with a fool's cap on, had time to fully realize the foolishness of his own behaviour.

Forest History and Arithmetic were the Badger's two favourite studies, and each pupil was expected to know the

"THE BEAR-MOTHER HAD LEARNT THE CONCERTINA IN ALL ITS BRANCHES"

Multiplication Table upside-down, and to be able to give the date of any event in Bear-history, without a moment's hesitation.

It was perhaps not to be wondered at that the scholars were glad when playtime arrived, and that they rushed home helter-skelter, with shouts of joy, the moment the School-house door was thrown open.

Many practical jokes had been tried upon the old School-master, and the offenders had invariably been severely punished, but one day in early autumn Knut and Otto, as they walked home with their friends, suggested a plan which would sweep away at one blow a great part of the misery of their School life.

"You know the great History and Arithmetic books that Herr Badger always keeps on the desk in front of him?" said Knut. "We'll scoop out the insides and fill them with fireworks. Then directly he comes into School, we'll let them off. What an explosion there'll be! He *will* be frightened! No more sums and dates after that. Hurrah! Hurrah!"

The scholars jumped about with delight when they heard the young Bears' idea, and eagerly agreed to join in the mischief.

Their mothers were quite surprised the next morning to see with what alacrity they all started for School—half-an-hour earlier than their usual custom—and Fru Bjornson remarked to her old servant that "she really believed the children were beginning to take an interest in their studies *at last !* "

The old Badger had not yet finished breakfast in his cottage by the School-house ; so his pupils were able to enter the School-room unobserved, and had soon carried out their simple arrangements.

An oiled string was attached, winding up the leg of the table to the fireworks ; and the end was to be lighted by Knut the moment Herr Badger had seated himself.

Everything being completed, the scholars seized their books ; and when their master appeared in the doorway, murmured a respectful greeting, to which he responded by a stately bow.

" Your slates, pupils. We will commence as usual with a few easy sums."

A subdued groan broke from the scholars ; and Knut— stooping down under pretence of tying up his shoe—applied a match to the string, while his companions shuffled as loudly as possible, to hide the sound of the striking.

" Silence, if you *please !* " shouted the Badger. " Have you come to school to dance the polka ? Attend to this little problem immediately, and mind it is correctly answered. If 10,000 Bears and a Pole-cat, ran round a tree 1,500 times and a half, in an hour and ten minutes ; each knocking off one leaf and three-quarters every time he ran round—how many leaves would be knocked off in a fortnight ? "

" They couldn't do it," muttered a hedgehog derisively.

"There wouldn't be room for a quarter of them!"
"Make haste! Make haste!" cried the Badger, rapping
his desk; but just at that moment, *whirr! whizz! bang!*
The books flew open with a loud report, and out sprang
the crackers, and began to fizz and bound about the table.

Herr Badger's black skull cap tumbled off, and he fell
backwards in his astonishment, shouting for help; while the
whole school darted away through the open door into the
woods, in a state of the wildest delight and excitement.

CHAPTER II.

Fru Bjornson was busily employed in her kitchen, stirring
up some liquid in a large saucepan. It was cranberry jam
for the winter, and on the floor stood a long row of brown
jars into which it was to be poured when the boiling was
thoroughly completed.

The servant. a little thin light-brown Bear, in a large
apron; waited close by, ready to poke the fire, or give any
other assistance that was required of her.

In the salon, Herr Bjornson, with a pucker on his forehead, was adding up his Bee accounts—for he kept a
number of hives in the garden and fields belonging to him.

Suddenly the alarm bell sounded loudly, and in rushed
the Bear-mother, with the jam-ladle in her hand, her hair
almost erect with terror.

"They have found us at last! What shall we do? Where shall we fly to?" she cried distractedly.

"Into the ice-cellar," cried Herr Bjornson, "come, Ingold. Everyone follow me!" and he threw his papers down on the ground and ran out at the back door.

Fortunately the ice-cellar was near the house, and the frightened family were soon safely in its shelter.

By opening a crack in the small trap-door, which was level with the ground, they were able to see all that went on in the garden; and the steps afforded them a place to sit down upon, without touching the great blocks of ice that looked white and ghostly as the thin streak of daylight struggled in upon them.

"Is anyone coming?" whispered the Bear-mother nervously.

"I can't see anything moving," growled Herr Bjornson. "Keep back, Mother. I can't help treading upon you. Dear me! How cramped we are here!"

"It's terribly cold," said the Bear-mother shivering. "I can feel myself freezing in every hair."

"Wrap your shawl round you, and stamp about a little."

Fru Bjornson attempted to carry out the directions, but the space was so small there was scarcely room to move in it.

The air seemed to get colder and colder; Ingold's fur turned frost-white, and she twined her apron round her head to prevent herself from being frost-bitten.

"Oh, this is awful," quaked the Bear-mother. "We shall all die or be turned into icicles if we can't get out before long!"

The Bear-father had put up his coat-collar and tied his bandanna pocket-handkerchief over his ears. His hair was also covered with white crystals, and he was seized with an attack of coughing which obliged him to borrow the Bear-mother's shawl to bury his head in, so that the sound might not be heard outside.

"This is painful in the extreme," he said in a choked voice as he emerged gasping. "A cough lozenge at this moment might be the saving of us!"

"What shall we do if the enemy hears us!" cried Fru Bjornson. "Here! I have just found a peppermint-drop in my pocket. Let us divide it into three. It may be some slight assistance."

They soon discovered, however, that lozenges were utterly powerless to keep out that biting air, and the Bear-mother seated herself resignedly on an ice-block.

"It's no good struggling against fate," she murmured. "We shall be found by the children, I suppose. You'd better keep your arms down straight, father; and freeze as narrow as possible. Then they will be able to get you out of the opening without much difficulty. It seems hard to think they will never know the true facts of the case," she continued mournfully. "Our epitaph will probably be 'Sat down carelessly in an Ice-house!'"

" Don't despair, Mother," cried Herr Bjornson, who had one eye anxiously applied to the crack in the trap-door. "I see the back gate opening. In another minute we shall know the worst—Hi! What! Well, I never! Who do you think it is, Mother? Why, *the Schoolmaster!* "

Herr Badger indeed it was, who had come off in a great hurry to complain of the disgraceful behaviour of his pupils, and being very excited had inadvertently trodden on the wire of the alarm bell as he entered the private grounds of the Bear-family.

He seemed a little surprised as the strange procession suddenly rose up out of the ground in front of him, but without making any enquiries as to what they had been doing there, he plunged at once into the history of his wrongs.

CHAPTER III.

All day the Badger's scholars enjoyed themselves in the forest. They played leap-frog, ran races, bathed in the river, had lunch in a shady hollow, and picked more cranberries than they knew what to do with; but as evening came on, they began to wonder a little anxiously whether the Schoolmaster would already have been round to their parents to complain of their behaviour; and when Knut and Otto entered their own door in the bushes, their knees were shaking under them, and it occurred to them that perhaps the fireworks hadn't been quite so amusing as they expected, after all!

They were met by Herr Bjornson with a gloomy frown. There was no doubt that Herr Badger had told him everything, and the little Bears waited tremblingly for what was to happen next.

"What is this that I hear?" commenced the Father-bear angrily. "Your respected Master ill-treated in his own School-house. Thrown violently upon the ground, with crackers exploding round him for several hours! What have you to say for yourselves?"

"Please, father, we didn't mean to hurt him," began Knut in a piping voice; "It was only to get rid of the books. We won't do it again!"

"I should think *not*, indeed," said Herr Bjornson. "I shall punish you myself severely to-morrow, after School time, and Herr Badger is going to give you two hours' extra Arithmetic every day for a fortnight."

Knut and Otto crept off miserably into the garden, and that evening there was no dancing, and the Bear-mother's concertina was silent.

Before it was daylight next morning, Knut had awakened Otto. They had determined the night before that they would *never* return to Herr Badger's rule, and the matter of the extra Arithmetic had settled their determination.

They started with their cloaks, and with lunch in their

satchels, as if going to School—leaving a note for their mother upon the kitchen dresser.

This letter was written with the stump of a lead pencil, and ran as follows :—

"*To the well-born Fru Bjornson.*

"*We cant keep at ilt any mor. We want to be inderpendent, and the sums are 2 mutch. We sik our fortones, and return wen we ar rich.*

"KNUT. OTTO."

As soon as they reached the forest, the two little Bears ran forward as quickly as they could towards the river.

They intended to take any canoe they found by the shore, and row themselves over to the opposite side. They did not know exactly what they should do when they got there ; but anyhow, they would be safe from punishment when they were once over.

As they went along they kept as much as possible behind the underwood, though it was so early it was scarcely likely that any of the charcoal-burners or fishermen would be stirring.

After some search they discovered a small canoe drawn up under the bushes, and untying it without much difficulty, they got in, and Knut paddled actively out into the strong current.

" This *is* independence ! " cried Otto, arranging the knap-sacks and cloaks in the bow of the boat, and taking up the steering-paddle. " What would Herr Badger say if he could see us now ? "—and he chuckled.

All day they drifted down the river—watching the salmon dart about the boulders, and the trout leap in the curling eddies. It was so silent in the great forest, with the pine trees growing close to the edge of the water, that at last the little Bears' high spirits began to fail them; and as the evening came on their laughter ceased, and they sat quietly in the canoe, steering their way between the great rocks without speaking.

" How strong the current is here," muttered Otto at last. " I can scarcely keep the boat straight ! "

" Well, let's land and find some place to sleep in," cried Knut—but this was more easily said than done. The moment they tried to turn the canoe in towards the shore, it began to whirl round and round ; and finally striking against a stone, it upset the two little Bears into the middle of the foaming river.

CHAPTER IV.

Fortunately Knut and Otto were good swimmers, and they were able after some struggling to scramble to the shore ; but they found to their great annoyance that they had landed on the same side as that from which they had started.

Their canoe was whirling rapidly away down the rapids, and it was useless to think of recovering it ; so the two little Bears proceeded to dry their clothes as well as they could, and then looked about to see if they could find a comfortable place to sleep in.

A large hollow tree stood close to the edge of the river, and into this they climbed, and being very tired they were soon fast asleep.

They were awakened by voices.

" It's *men !* " whispered Otto, clutching Knut's arm in terror. " Oh, why did we ever run away ! They'll be *sure* to find us ! "

" Be quiet, Otto," muttered Knut. " Do you want them to hear ? Lie still, and I'll think of some way to escape."

" Are you sure this is the right tree ? " said a man's voice.

" Don't you see the mark ? " asked another. " The Forester put it on himself; though it's rather high up. You'd better begin work at once, or you'll not get through with it before he comes round again."

This was awful. Otto trembled so that he could hear his own teeth chattering ; but Knut kept his presence of mind, and poking his brother warningly, said in a hoarse whisper,

" Wait till I give the signal, and then jump out after me as high in the air as you can. Follow me till I tell you to stop.''

An echoing blow resounded against the tree trunk, which made Knut fly up like a sky-rocket.

"Now!" he cried, and bounding on to the edge of the opening, he jumped right over the heads of the woodmen into the tangled bushes, followed by Otto, and away they raced through the forest, before the astonished men could recover themselves.

"What in the world was that?" cried the wood-cutters, rubbing their eyes and blinking; but no one had been able to see more than two flying brown balls, and after hunting about in vain, they decided it must have been a couple of gigantic owls.

Only one thing did they find in the hollow tree, and that certainly puzzled them—a small piece of crumpled paper, on which was sketched a life-like picture of a Badger with a fool's cap on his head; underneath, written in cramped letters—

"*How would you like it?*"

After running for about half an hour, Knut sank down panting on a juniper bush, while Otto rolled upon the moss thoroughly exhausted.

"Arithmetic was better than this!" he panted dismally, fanning himself with a large fern leaf. "History was better—*anything* was better!"

"Well, we're quite safe here for the present," replied Knut, "so don't worry yourself any more. I'm so tired I can't keep awake, and I'm sure you can't." And, indeed, in spite of their fright, in a few minutes both the little Bears were sound asleep again.

N

When they next opened their eyes, the sun was glinting through the pine trees; and looking down on them benignly, stood a Fox in travelling dress, with a soft felt hat upon his head.

He smiled graciously upon Knut, and beckoned him to come out of the juniper bushes.

"Ha! ha! my good gentlemen, you are taking a comfortable rest in a very secluded spot, but you can't escape *my* observation!" he cried cheerfully. "Are you on your way to some foreign Court—or perhaps you are couriers with State secrets?"

The two little Bears, feeling very flattered, sat up and straightened their tunics.

"The truth is, we are seeking our fortunes," said Knut with dignity.

"Oh, nothing easier," replied the Fox. "You come with me. Such hearty, well-grown young Bears will find no difficulty in getting excellent situations. I can almost promise you each a large income if you implicitly follow my directions."

"Where should we go to, then?" asked Knut cautiously.

"To a dear friend of mine, who employs an immense number of workmen," said the Fox easily. "I will just let you see who I am before we proceed further," and he drew a case from his pocket, and taking out a card, presented it to the little Bears with a low bow.

The Badger's School. 193

"Just as if we were grown up!" whispered Otto. "Oh, Knut, how different this is to Herr Badger!"

On the card, printed in elegant copper-plate, was the following—

"*Herr Kreutzen, Under-Secretary (and Working Member) of the Society for promoting the welfare of Farmers.*"

Knut looked at Herr Kreutzen respectfully.

"If you'll be so kind as to show us the way, we'll follow you at once," he said. "If we could get a little breakfast on the way, we should be glad; for we have lost our satchels, and berries are not very satisfying."

"Come along, then!" said the Fox briskly; and seizing the two little Bears by the paw, he dragged them into the heart of the forest at a rapid pace.

CHAPTER V.

On the day after his visit to the Bjornson family, Herr Badger, feeling very dull, sat alone in the cottage by the School-house.

Every one of his pupils had deserted him; for not only had the two little Bears run away, but all their companions had also played truant; and the whole of that part of the forest was filled with parents anxiously searching for their missing children—like a gigantic game of hide-and-seek.

Herr Badger called to his housekeeper to bring him the

black-board, a couple of globes, and the book of conic-
sections, and for some hours he amused himself happily ;
but at the end of that time he began to experience an
almost irresistible desire to teach something.

"If I can't get anyone else, I'll call Brita," he said to
himself. " I can just ask her a few easy questions suited
to her limited intellect."

The housekeeper came in, curtsying respectfully, and
seated herself at the table, as she was bidden.

" I must imagine I have given up school, and taken to
private pupils," the Badger said to himself. " I hope she
won't exasperate me, and make me lose my temper ! Now
take this slate," he continued aloud, " and try and do one
of these simple sums. You'll soon get used to them—

" If five onions were to be boiled in six saucepans, how
would you divide the onions so that there would be exactly
the same quantity in each pan ? "

" Chop them up," replied the housekeeper promptly.

The Badger glared. " You're not attending. I said,
' How would you *divide* them ! ' "

" You might mince them very fine, or pound them in a
mortar," replied the housekeeper anxiously. " I don't know
of no other way of doing it."

" Work it out on the slate, creature !—on the *slate !* "
cried Herr Badger, thumping the table with his long ruler.

" I'd rather do it on a dish, sir," said the housekeeper,
trembling. " It's more what I'm accustomed to."

Herr Badger started up in a fury. " *You* call yourself a private pupil ? " he shouted (quite forgetting that the housekeeper had never called herself anything of the kind). " Go back to the kitchen immediately."

" I could bring you the Mole who blacks the boots, if *he'd* be any good," said the housekeeper humbly. " I know I'm very ignorant, but the Mole tells me he's been attending day school for years, and he reads recipes out of the cookery-book quite beautiful."

" Don't speak to me of Moles ! " said the Badger crossly. " I shall take no more private pupils—they're not worth it." And he walked over to the black-board, and began to draw diagrams.

" What's the good of diagrams, without a class to explain them to ? " he muttered. " I declare I believe I *was* too hard on those children. We can't be all equally gifted. It wouldn't be a bad idea if I went out as one of the search parties. I declare I *will !* " he continued, his face brightening, " and I'll make every creature I find promise to come back to school again. I must make up a class somehow, or I shall die of monotony."

He took down his old felt hat with the ear-flaps, and putting some food in a knapsack, and choosing a stout walking-stick, he flung a green cloak over his shoulders, and let himself out into the forest.

CHAPTER VI.

The Fox took the two little Bears on so quickly, that they soon began to feel both cross and tired. To their anxious enquiries as to where they were going, and whether they could not soon have some breakfast, Herr Kreutzen answered vaguely that they would very soon reach their destination, and should have as much breakfast as they could possibly care for.

"My friends are kind worthy people, and you'll find every sort of luxury," he said, smiling benignly.

"We seem to be coming near a town," whispered Knut to Otto. "I don't quite like this!" and he tried to pull his paw away from the good "Secretary of the Society for promoting the welfare of Farmers."

"Come along, my dear child. We are almost there," cried the Fox. "I am just going to tie you both up to this tree for a minute—merely to be sure you are quite safe and happy in my absence—and I shall return with my kind friend, in no time!"

Herr Kreutzen took some string from his pocket as he spoke, and the two little Bears—who saw there was no use in struggling—submitted to be fastened together to a fir tree.

As soon as the Fox had disappeared, Otto burst into a loud roar of terror.

"Oh, he's going to do something dreadful, I know he is! We shall never, *never* get away again!"

"It's no good making that noise," said Knut, angrily. "Leave off, Otto, and let me think."

"You may think for ever," wailed Otto, "and unless you've got a pocket knife you won't get these knots undone!" and he began to cry again with renewed vigour.

"Why, whatever is the matter?" said a friendly voice close by.

The little Bears looked round eagerly, and saw that an elderly Badger was approaching. He was evidently a wood-cutter, for he had a large axe in his hand, and the three young Badgers who followed him were carrying neatly-tied bundles of sticks.

Knut stretched out his paw beseechingly.

"*Please* cut the string! Oh, *please*, Herr Badger, make haste, and let us get free. Herr Kreutzen will be back in a minute, and then there'll be *no* hope for us!"

"So this is some of *his* work!" said the Badger angrily. "I declare that creature is a plague to the whole forest!"

With two blows of his axe he cut the strings that bound the little Bears; and ordering them to follow him to a place of safety, he darted through the bushes with his children, and never stopped until they came out into a secluded valley, at the end of which, in a small clearing, stood a hut built of pine logs.

Before the door sat the Badger-mother with some plain sewing, while five of the young Badger-children played about on the grass in front of her.

"You're home early to-day, father," she said cheerfully, and added, as she caught sight of the little Bears—" Why, wherever did you pick up these strangers, father ?"

The Badger described the unpleasant position in which he had found them; and the whole family gathering round, Knut related their adventures truthfully from the very beginning.

"I'll tell you where the Fox was taking you, my children," said the Badger-mother; "There's a Wild Beast Show in the town at this present moment, and Herr Kreutzen has already enticed two or three animals into it. He is well paid by the showman, and would have made a good thing out of you, because you could have been taught to dance. Oh, what a miserable fate you have escaped from !"

Knut and Otto looked thoroughly ashamed of themselves, and began to realize what their foolishness might have led them into.

However, no one could be miserable for long at a time in the Badger family; they were all so happy and light-hearted—so after a good dinner, the two little Bears ran out into the garden, and forgot their troubles in a romp with the children.

"You did not know your old schoolmaster was a cousin of ours?" remarked the Badger-mother, as they rested, later on, under a shady fir tree. "He really is a worthy creature at heart, and you ought all to try and put up with him as much as possible."

"We really _will_," cried the two little Bears heartily. "If ever we get back again, we really _will!_" and they thoroughly intended to keep their promises.

"I think this evening you should start for home before it grows dusk," said the Badger-mother. "Father will see you well on your way, and your parents must be longing to hear of you. Come into the house now, and I will make you look respectable."

Knut and Otto were all obedience, and followed the Badger-mother meekly to the kitchen. Here she took down two large scrubbing-brushes, and proceeded to give them a thorough tidying. Then their faces were soaped, and finally two of the young Badgers' caps were placed upon their heads—for their own had fallen off when they were upset into the river.

The elastics were very tight under their chins, but they refrained from saying anything—and this showed how complete was their reformation!

Just as all the preparations were completed, there came a loud knock at the door; and the Schoolmaster himself appeared, his clothes torn, one flap off his hat, a bandage covering his right eye, leading in a little crowd of scholars that he had collected with infinite toil from many perilous positions.

There were two Hedgehogs, a young Fox, five Badgers, a Mole, and a tame Guinea-pig. All of them were more or less scratched, and dismal looking; and some had evidently

been in the water, for their clothes were still dripping, and
hung round them in the most uncomfortable manner.

"What! *you* here, after all! Well, this *is* a happy
meeting!" cried Herr Badger, embracing the little Bears
warmly. "I wasn't going home till I'd found you—and
here you are. A most fortunate coincidence!"

"Sit down, sit down, cousin," said the Badger-mother
hospitably. "Bring in the pupils, and let them dry their
hair before the fire—they seem in a sad state, poor things!"

"They certainly *do* look a little untidy," said the Badger,
"but we shall soon remedy all that. I have been explaining
to the class (at least to as much as I've got of it)," he continued, turning to Knut, "that the plan of the School is to
be entirely reformed—ten minutes' Arithmetic per day, and
History *once* weekly. What do you say to that, children?"

A feeble cheer arose from the pupils; and the two little
Bears, throwing themselves upon their knees, begged their
Master's pardon for all the trouble they had caused him.

CHAPTER VII.

Fru Bjornson, seated on a camp-stool by the side of the
entrance gate to her house, was looking anxiously around
her. Close by stood Ingold, with one eye tightly screwed
up, and an old-fashioned telescope in her hand, trying in
vain to adjust the focus.

"What do you see now?" enquired the Bear-mother, leaning forward.

"A great fog with snakes in it!" replied the servant truthfully.

"Why, those are *trees*, of course!" said Fru Bjornson. "Turn the screw a little more, and it will become as plain as possible."

Ingold twisted her hand several times rapidly, and again applied her eye to the end.

"It doesn't seem like snakes now, does it?" asked the Bear-mother triumphantly.

"Oh, no! It's turned to milk with green splashes in it," said Ingold.

"You don't see anything of my darling children, then?" enquired Fru Bjornson.

"Nothing at all, ma'am," said Ingold. "A telescope may be a wonderful thing for those who haven't any eyes, but really I think *I* see better *without* it."

At this moment, through the trees, an extraordinary procession came in sight; which caused the Bear-mother to jump up from her seat with a cry of joy.

Herr Badger, with his cloak thrown over one shoulder, leading Knut and Otto by the hand; and behind them the rest of the pupils in single file—depressed and gloomy, but resigned to whatever Fate might have in store for them.

Fru Bjornson ran forward, and clasped her children in her arms.

It was a happy meeting; and as she thought the School-master would already have gone through all the scolding that was necessary, she refrained from adding a word more.

"I've got the class together, ma'am," said Herr Badger triumphantly, "and I'm never going to let it go again! The new School system commences from to-morrow!"

  *   *   *   *   *   *

All the parents agreed that the children had been suffi-ciently punished during their wanderings in the forest, and they were therefore allowed to return to their homes, without anything more being said on the subject.

The next morning the scholars assembled at the School-house in excellent time; but most of them unfortunately, having lost their satchels, were obliged to carry their books and luncheon, wrapped up in untidy brown paper parcels—which was certainly very mortifying.

"My dear pupils," commenced Herr Badger, as he entered the room and bowed graciously, "on this auspicious occa-sion, I wish to call the Arithmetic class for ten minutes only. We will begin, if you please, with 'twice one'—repeating it three times over *without a failure!*"

Bobbie's Two Shillings.

A GUINEA-PIG STORY.

CHAPTER I.

N a sloping lawn, before an old-fashioned, rambling house, Bobbie and Jerry were playing at nine-pins on a hot day in August.

Under the shade of a cedar tree the under-nurse sat working; and "Aunt Lucy"—an old lady with snow-white hair, crowned by a black mushroom hat—was slowly pacing the gravel walk, digging out a weed here and there with a long spud she carried for the purpose.

Jerry was only playing nine-pins because Bobbie was so fond of them. She did not care for them herself, for she thought that as she was ten years old they were too babyish, but Bobbie was only eight, so of course it was not to be expected of him that he would care for "grown-up" things.

There was a pleasant buzzing in the air, as old Jeptha Funnel led the donkey in the mowing machine, up and down the wide lawn, pausing every now and then to exchange a few words with the children.

" When are you a-coming to tea with us, Master Bobbie,
and Missy ? " he enquired, stopping to fan his heated face
with a red pocket-handkerchief. " James Seton's got some
guinea-pigs that he talks of bringing over for you to see, any
day as you'll fix upon."

" Oh, that *is* nice.   I do so long to have another ! " cried
Bobbie rapturously.   " I only want three-halfpence-farthing
more, and I shall have enough in my money-box to pay for
it.   Will James wait till Friday ? "

" Of course he will, Master Bobbie ; don't you worry your
head about that."

" Well, it's an extraordinary thing, Jeptha, but you can't
think how I've been saving, and saving, and *saving* for that
guinea-pig ; and it seems as if I never *should* have enough,"
said Bobbie confidentially.   " I saved up for ' Funnel '—the
one that's called after you, you know—in no time ; but we
were up in Scotland then, and there wasn't hardly any
shops that I *could* spend my money in."

" Things always *do* seem a long time a-coming when
you're longing for them, so to speak, day and night, sir."

" Yes, it's quite true that ' a watch-pocket never boils,'" said
Bobbie.   " I shall leave off rattling the money-box, and try
and forget all about it till Friday."

" You're right there, sir," said Jeptha, not noticing the new
rendering of the proverb, for he was as fond of long words
and sentences as Bobbie himself; " you come right up to
the cottage on Friday, along of nurse and Miss Jerry.   The

missus 'll have tea for you, and *I'll* see that Jim brings the guinea-pigs."

" Does James Seton know anything about cats ? " enquired Jerry eagerly. " You know they're *my* favourite animals— just like guinea-pigs are Bobbie's—and I do want to get some new recipes for my cat-book ! "

" Why whatever is a cat-book, Miss Jerry ? " asked Jeptha curiously.

" Don't you know, Jeptha ? I write down all sorts of cures for cats, and what they ought to eat ; and several times it's been very useful to Miss Meadows and Maria."

" I can't say *I* know much about the subject, Miss Jerry, nor I don't think Jim doesn't, neither, never having made a study of it, as you may say. Miss Meadders is the tabby cat, ain't she ? A very fine cat I call her."

" Yes ; I made a portrait of her and Maria, to send to mamma out in India, and Bobbie made a picture of Funnel (not *you*, you know). She liked them so much. Shall I tell you why Bobbie is so interested in guinea-pigs ? " continued Jerry, taking the old man's hand, and speaking in a mysterious whisper.

" You know Jack belongs to the ' Cavey Club ' at school, where all the boys *must* keep guinea-pigs ; and he wrote Bobbie a letter last term with a picture of a guinea-pig on the flap of the envelope, and ' Where is it ? ' written where the tail ought to be. Ever since then Bobbie has been *mad* after guinea-pigs."

"Yes, I can remember Master Jack a-walking in here with ten of 'em," said Jeptha, "and keepin' 'em in the lumber room in houses made out of cigar-boxes."

"Oh, but Aunt Lucy found it out, and wouldn't allow it," said Jerry. "They all had to be taken out to the stable yard again."

"I must own I think on *that* occasion yer Aunt was reasonable, Miss Jerry; a guinea-pig don't seem a kind of a domestic indoor animal—like a cat, for instance."

"Will you have mufflings and crumfits for tea, do you think, when we come?" enquired Bobbie, after a thoughtful pause. "Escuse me asking you, but I do like them so very much."

"Oh, Bobbie, you shouldn't say that!" cried Jerry, reprovingly; "it's very impolite. Aunt Lucy would be quite *horrified!*"

"Well, I don't *mean* anything rude," said Bobbie. "I *do* like them, and I can't help it. I can't see why it's any more rude than if I said I liked guinea-pigs."

CHAPTER II.

The next day was a very wet one; and Aunt Lucy, coming up into the schoolroom in the morning—as she invariably did, even during the holidays—saw a most extraordinary collection of baskets standing on the floor, in front of a small fire of sticks blazing away in the fireplace.

There was a large covered market basket, a fish bag with a skewer through the top, and a small japanese basket, with a lid which was kept in place by the poker and tongs laid carefully over it.

The baskets were all occasionally agitated from within; and Aunt Lucy found on enquiry that they contained the guinea-pig family, who having been flooded out of their usual quarters by the rain, had been brought in to a fire by Bobbie to be dried!

"I really object to these animals in the house!" said Aunt Lucy, trying to be severe; but Bobbie's face was so pathetic, she did not order them to be taken out at once, as she had at first intended.

"As soon as they are dry you must move them away, Bobbie," she continued; "I have had quite enough trouble with Jack's. I can't have the house turned into a menagerie."

"Really, Aunt Lucy, you needn't mind Habbakuk and Funnel—they are so very well behaved. I *have* been debillerating whether I ought to bring in Pompey, because his hair *streams* out—but he did look so cold and mis'rable, I thought you wouldn't objec'."

At this moment a housemaid came up to say there were visitors in the drawing-room.

"It is your two uncles from India," said Aunt Lucy, taking Bobbie's reluctant hand. "They have come on purpose to see you, so you must leave the guinea-pigs for

o

a minute—Jerry can stay with them, and come down as
soon as you return."

Bobbie departed groaning, while the under-nurse good-
naturedly made up the fire, and began to dry the guinea-
pigs with an old duster.

In a few minutes Bobbie returned, his fat round face red
with the exertion of scrambling upstairs, his brown eyes
sparkling.

"What are they like?" enquired Jerry, who was not fond
of visitors, as Anne brushed at her curly hair, and tried in
vain to flatten it to the nursery regulation of smoothness.

"Oh, two middle-aged, light gentlemen," replied Bobbie
carelessly. "One gave me a shilling to buy a guinea-pig,
so now I'm quite safe in telling James to bring them on
Friday." And Bobbie seated himself before the fire with
Habbakuk and Funnel on his knees, and rubbed away at
them vigorously.

Jerry retired downstairs, but reappeared in a very short
time—rushing into the room again like a whirlwind.

"What do you think the uncles have promised us,
Bobbie?" she cried excitedly; "guess the most beautifullest
thing you can possibly think of!"

"Guin——" commenced Bobbie, and checked himself
hastily.

"Certainly not!" said Jerry, with decision. "I said I
must run up and tell you, you'd be so *wild* with joy; it
begins with a ' P '—but it isn't ' pig.' Now guess again."

" Prawns, p'rambulators, prongs, pastry," commenced
Bobbie rapidly. " Well, none of those are very nice except
pastry. I can't think of anything more, Jerry, you *must*
tell me."

"Pantomime!" said Jerry, triumphantly; "*next Saturday!*
—what do you say to that ?"

Bobbie's eyes twinkled. " With preserved seats, like we
had last time! Oh, splendid!" and he began to caper
about the room with delight.

"Well, this *has* been a day!" he exclaimed, as he sank
down, quite exhausted. "What a lot for my diary! I'd
better write it out at once, before I forget it."

A large book, interleaved with blotting-paper, was dis-
interred from the play-box, and Bobbie sat down before it
solemnly.

The greater part of this book was filled with minute
accounts of what time its owner got up, and went to bed,
what pudding he had for dinner, and what lessons he learnt;
but on this occasion the entry assumed such large proportions
that it spread right over the next day, and was wandering
into " Friday," when Bobbie suddenly remembered the tea-
party, and that room must certainly be left for *that!*

Jerry, looking over his shoulder, when he had finished,
read the following, adorned with many blots and smudges :—

" Had sutch a day. 2 lite gentlemen who turnered into
Unkels (' You mean, " turned *out* to be uncles," ' corrected
Jerry) came And gave me 1 shiling for the brown ginny-pig

I acepted with thanks they are goin to tak us Jerry and me to the pantermine and tea at Mrs. Funnels on Fryday (not the Unkels but nurs).

" P.S.—Plenty mor to say but no rume. cant put the puding today."

CHAPTER III.

One of Bobbie's and Jerry's greatest treats was to have tea at the cottage on the edge of the park, where old Mrs. Funnel presided over a table covered with cakes and home-made delicacies.

She always liked them to appear in good time; so punctually at four o'clock on Friday, the invited tea-party—consisting of " Old Nurse," in a crackling black silk, Jerry in spotless frilled cotton, and Bobbie in a white sailor's suit, bristling with starch and pearl buttons—made their way through the little garden of the Funnels' house, and rapped importantly on the door with the end of nurse's umbrella.

Mrs. Funnel, who had been awaiting the summons, welcomed them heartily; and Bobbie was relieved to see— on taking a cursory glance at the table—that besides the usual array of good things, there was a covered dish, which meant, as he knew by experience—muffins.

Jeptha, in his Sunday coat, with a red geranium in his button-hole, looked cheerfully conscious of his own splendour ; and his wife's little wrinkled face beamed with kindness and hospitality.

"Jim can't get away yet, I'm sorry to say," she said, "but he'll be in afterwards. Sit down, all of you, please. Draw up to the table, ma'am ! "

Bobbie deposited his dog-skin gloves carefully in his hat, and seated himself solemnly, trying to keep his eyes off the plum cake, for the sake of good manners.

"This bread's a bit heavy, mother ! " remarked Jeptha, grappling with a large loaf in the centre of the table.

"I don't know how that can be," replied Mrs. Funnel cheerfully. " It rose enough."

"Then it must ha' sat down again !" said Jeptha. "It's that worritting oven, ma'am "—turning to nurse ; " I assure you we *do* have a time with it sometimes."

The tea began merrily, and just in the middle of it the door opened, and James Seton's sunburnt face looked in. He carried a basket which Bobbie pounced upon eagerly, for he knew it contained the long-expected guinea-pigs.

Behind Jim stood a little woe-begone creature in a ragged dress, her head covered by a large crumpled sun-bonnet. The tears were rolling down her face, and in her hand she held the bottom of a broken glass medicine bottle.

" Look here, grandmother," said Jim, " I picked up this unfort'net little mortal just outside the Lodge gates. She'd been into town to buy some lotion for her sick mother, and she went and fell up against a stone, and smashed her bottle; and now she's in a terrible state of mind about it."

The little girl was still crying bitterly; and Bobbie, who was very tender-hearted, furtively wiped his eyes with the back of his hand, and looked hard out of the window.

"Sit you down, child, and have some tea. You're fair worn out with misery," said Mrs. Funnel kindly. "After that we'll think of what's to be done. How much did the medicine cost, child?"

"Two shillings," said the child, with a fresh burst of sobbing.

Bobbie discovered, to his great annoyance, that two large tears had fallen down his own cheeks out of sympathy; and at the same moment he seemed to feel his little wash-leather purse growing so large, that he almost fancied in another moment it would burst out of his pocket.

Exactly two shillings were in it—the price of the bottle of lotion, or of two of Jim's guinea-pigs! Which should it be?

"If only I hadn't bought Maria's collar last Monday, I could have got you a bottle *easily*," cried Jerry, in great distress. "I've only twopence-halfpenny left, but *do* take it. Oh, you poor little girl, I *am* so sorry for you!"

Bobbie felt very guilty, and his money seemed to weigh upon him like lead. He watched the attractive brown guinea-pigs—who had been let out of their basket—gambol about the parlour. His mind was a chaos.

Suddenly he snatched out his purse, and thrust the two

shillings into the little girl's hand, before she could say anything.

"Get the medicine, please," he said, in a gruff voice. "I don't want the guinea-pigs, thank you, Jim." And opening the door hurriedly, he darted off across the park towards home.

CHAPTER IV.

"I do think it was one of the goodest things I ever heard of," said Jerry confidentially, as she drove with one of the "light gentlemen" to the pantomime.

She had just finished an account of Bobbie's heroic sacrifice of the day before; and as Bobbie himself was following in a hansom cab, with the other uncle, it was quite safe to relate the whole story without fear of interruptions.

"He wanted those guinea-pigs *dreadfully*," continued Jerry, "and he gave everything he had to the poor little girl. He cried horribly about it, though. He was literally *roaring* when we got back from Mrs. Funnel's tea, though he went and hid himself so that we shouldn't know; but nurse said his blouse was quite *damp!*"

"Shall we go round on our way back, and order Bobbie some new guinea-pigs, as a surprise?" asked Uncle Ronald, who had listened to the story with all the respectful sympathy expected of him.

Jerry gave a shriek of delight. " Oh, how *lovely !* May I choose ? I know just his favourite colours."

As Bobbie took his usual stroll into the stable yard on Monday morning, he was astonished to see Jeptha approaching him with a large box on a wheelbarrow.

" Summut for you, Master Bobbie. Come by rail; and there seems to be a deal of moving about and squeaking a-goin' on inside ! "

Bobbie unfastened the covers with feverish haste ; and there was a hutch such as he had never even *dreamt* of, with a row of four little eager noses sticking out between the bars.

A label hanging to the wire said, " From the two light gentlemen."

" Well now, Master Bobbie, if ever I saw the like of that!" cried Jeptha admiringly. " Why, they're all a-sittin' as comfortable as you please, in a kind of a Eastern palace."

Bobbie, who was almost delirious with delight and excitement, ran in to fetch Jerry.

" Oh, Jerry, come out ! " he cried. " The light gentlemen—in a splendid blue cage with red stripes, come by train ! And such guinea-pigs ! Just the kind I wanted— two long-hair. Oh, I do think this is the splendidest day of my life, and as long as I live I won't never forget it ! "